I0819472

ALICE'S COUNTRY DIARY QUILT

ALICE'S COUNTRY DIARY QUILT

A QUILTING JOURNEY THROUGH THE SEASONS WITH ENGLISH PAPER PIECING AND HAND EMBROIDERY

Alice Caroline

DAVID & CHARLES
— PUBLISHING —

www.davidandcharles.com

Contents

Introduction

I am delighted to introduce you to my Alice's Country Diary Quilt. This double-bed sized heirloom quilt comprises twenty-five beautiful blocks, each featuring a hand-embroidered design from nature, displayed within a circular patchwork frame created using the hand-stitched English paper piecing (EPP) technique. A further twelve half ring EPP border blocks complete this wonderful quilt.

The creative journey for Alice's Country Diary Quilt began during the COVID-19 pandemic, initiated by the more frequent local countryside walks I took during the lockdowns. I love wildflowers and thought I knew a fair few, until I started to really take notice of the plants in the hedgerows and woodlands of my surrounding area. I began to see things that were new to me, opening up a whole other world, one that had always been there but that I had never taken the time to see.

I started researching plant names, finding out about their medicinal uses, learning which ones were edible, and discovering those that could be used to make natural dyes, which I also dabbled in. Our ancestors would have known all of these things as second nature, of course! This period of slow-living was not only the opportunity to explore the immediate world around me, but it also gave me the chance to re-engage with embroidery, which I had loved as a teenager.

This mindful slow-stitching technique seemed to me to be the perfect medium for capturing my observations from nature, and so I began to develop a series of embroideries that celebrated wildflowers through the seasons as well as the insects that flitted around them. I have shared some of my field notes about the flora and fauna featured in these designs in The Embroideries chapter, and I hope you enjoy learning about them as much as I did!

Thank you so much for joining me on this journey – let's get started! The Tools & Materials chapter outlines everything you will need to complete the quilt, then turn to Preparing to Begin for what you need to know before you pick up your sewing needle, with advice on how best to approach the making of the quilt. There are dedicated chapters, too, on both the EPP and embroidery techniques, offering step-by-step advice for those who need it, and easy-to-use transfers are included for each of the embroidery designs at the back of the book so you can get started straight away. I am so excited to be sharing this with you!

DISPOSITION DES FEUILLES
ARTHROPODES

Tools & Materials

In this chapter all the tools you require to make Alice's Country Diary Quilt are outlined in detail, from general equipment to those requirements specific to the EPP and embroidery techniques. Also, there is detailed information for the type and quantity of fabrics needed, as well as a complete thread list for the embroidery designs.

GENERAL EQUIPMENT

Rotary cutter and cutting mat: Using these will make it easier to cut lots of fabric shapes faster. Make sure the blades of your rotary cutter are sharp and check that your cutting mat is not highly scarred, as this can catch the fabric causing it to snag; also, the rotary cutter may slip into these channels, resulting in a cut not quite where you intended it to be.

Fabric scissors: If you prefer to use scissors for fabric cutting, take care when picking up the fabric not to shift things out of place.

Iron and ironing board: For transferring the iron-on embroidery transfers to the background fabric, and for pressing the finished blocks. When pressing the finished embroideries, always place right side down on top of a soft, fluffy towel and press from the back, to prevent damage to any textural stitches.

Needle threader: This optional piece of equipment can come in very useful when hand sewing.

Cutting template shapes are also available for the EPP from alicecaroline.com. Made from clear acrylic with seam allowance included, these are ideal for those who like to fussy cut their fabrics.

EPP EQUIPMENT

Tracing paper, paper and paper scissors: For tracing off and cutting out the EPP templates provided (see Preparing to Begin). We recommend a paper with a weight of at least 120gsm (80lb). Alternatively, an acrylic cutting template set or a bag of pre-cut paper shapes can be purchased from our website, www.alicecaroline.com.

Sewing thread: When sewing together the EPP fabric shapes, our recommendation would be to use a neutral cream or off-white thread colour, although you can colour match your thread to the fabric being sewn if you prefer. We have used Aurifil 50wt cotton thread but a Gütermann Sew-All 100% polyester or 100% cotton thread is also an option. A large spool is a good idea!

Hand sewing needle: A sharp, longer needle makes sewing easier. Choose a size 9–11 (the smaller the number, the longer the needle), making sure that the eye of the needle is not so small that it punctures your finger. Gold-tipped needles are also a great choice as they will glide through the fabric easily without tugging or snagging.

Thimble: If you prefer to use a thimble when sewing, choose one that fits well and is comfy to use. It should almost feel like it is part of your finger and a natural fit leather thimble can be a good choice.

Soluble fabric glue pen: This is used to hold the fabric shapes in place around the paper shapes required for EPP and we recommend the Sewline fabric glue pen (refills are available). Alternatively, if you prefer to use pins, small-headed ones are best.

Starch: This is used to press the finished full and half ring sections of EPP for a lovely crisp finish. Use a clean cloth or heat-resistant mat to protect the fabric, and make sure your iron is clean before you begin!

EMBROIDERY EQUIPMENT

Embroidery hoop, 6in (15.2cm) diameter: This keeps the fabric smooth and taut, making it much easier to stitch evenly and prevent puckers forming between stitches.

Screwdriver or pliers: These will help you tighten the screw on your embroidery hoop; one or the other will be more suitable depending on the hardware on your hoop.

Erasable pen or marker: Always test on a sample of your fabric first.

Embroidery needle: These have a long slender eye for threading thicker threads, a slightly thinner shaft, and a sharp point to pierce the fabric easily. Generally size 8–10 will be most suitable (the higher the number, the finer the needle); however, we recommend that you buy a mixed pack – Tulip Hiroshima needles are good – to see which size is most comfortable for you.

Small scissors: These should be sharp and pointed for snipping embroidery threads.

Thread organiser and magnifying glass: Optional extras, a thread organiser is an excellent way to keep your embroidery threads sorted and tangle-free, while a magnifying glass helps you to see the detail of the embroidery stitching.

QUILT MAKING EQUIPMENT

Sewing machine: With a standard sewing foot; a walking foot or a free-motion quilting foot (if machine quilting) can also be useful.

Hand quilting needle: We recommend using a 'sharp' or 'between' quilting needle; gold-tipped is best.

FABRICS

The minimum fabric requirements for making Alice's Country Diary Quilt with a finished size of 68 x 68in (172 x 172cm) are given here. For the cutting lists for the EPP and background fabrics, refer to Preparing to Begin: Fabric Cutting Lists.

EPP FABRIC

All printed fabrics used in this quilt are Liberty Tana Lawn® fabrics, a high quality 100% cotton fabric with a silk-like feel. Tana Lawn® is perfect for EPP due to the high thread count of the fabric, which enables the fine detail in each of the delicate designs. This lightweight fabric is really easy to work with by hand, but any lightweight 100% cotton quilting fabric can be used. The outer rings of each EPP block use sixteen fabrics specifically chosen for their bolder colours, arranged into stunning rainbows that repeat throughout the quilt (these are numbered 1 to 16 in the Block Layout Guides chapter). For the inner ring of each of the EPP blocks, just one soft, pastel shade is chosen from across thirteen different fabrics, to better allow the rainbow EPP ring to stand out and to ensure that the beautiful embroidery remains the focal point of each block (these are numbered X1 to X13 in the Block Layout Guides chapter). Refer to the Fabric Colour Chart for a colour shade guide when selecting your rainbow and pastel fabrics.

Rainbow fabrics 1–16: Minimum 13 x 22in (33 x 55.8cm) each.

Pastel fabric X10: Minimum 7 x 22in (17.8 x 55.8cm).

Pastel fabrics X1–X9 and X11–X13: Minimum 10 x 22in (25.4 x 55.8cm) each.

BACKGROUND FABRIC

The background fabric is used both for the block assembly and for the embroideries. White, ivory or off-white are all perfect choices. A lightweight 100% cotton fabric with some body, such as quilting cotton, is best, although you may also wish to use embroidery stabiliser to back the embroidery squares. (We do not recommend the use of cotton lawn for the background fabric as it is not thick enough to be embroidered on, even with added embroidery stabiliser.)

Background fabric: Minimum 256 x 44in (650 x 112cm).

FABRICS FOR QUILT FINISHING

For the backing fabric and binding, 100% cotton lightweight fabrics such as lawn or quilting cotton are best. For the wadding (batting), we recommend using a white or off-white wadding, such as Hobbs Heirloom 80/20 cotton/poly or 100% cotton.

Backing fabric: Minimum 78 x 78in (198 x 198cm). For 44in (112cm) or 54in (137cm) wide fabrics, cut two pieces 78in (198cm) long x width of fabric and sew them together to make a piece large enough for the backing.

Wadding: Minimum 78 x 78in (198 x 198cm).

Binding fabric: Minimum either 11 x 54in (28 x 137cm) or 13 x 44in (33 x 112cm). Cut the fabric into as many 1¾in (4.4cm) wide strips as possible, then sew these strips together end to end to make one long strip at least 288in (731cm) long. Then cut this strip down into four pieces of equal length ready for use. If you wish to use pre-made bias binding instead, you will need at least 7¾ yards (7 metres).

EMBROIDERY THREADS

For all the embroidery on Alice's Country Diary Quilt we have used DMC Mouliné Spécial, the world's favourite stranded embroidery thread. Forty different coloured threads have been used in total, although for most no more than one 8-metre skein is required. There are six strands of thread in each skein which are easily separated to allow for variations in the thickness and depth of the stitches (see Embroidery Techniques: Embroider the Designs).

TIP:

DMC threads are made to be colourfast and our own test results have supported this. However, you may pre-wash the threads if desired. Mix one tablespoon of white vinegar with one cup (240ml) of water and soak one skein of thread at a time. If the thread has any excess dye in it, the water will change colour. After soaking, take the thread out of the water/vinegar mixture and make sure it is completely dry before using.

1 SKEIN

14	502	895	3756
18	505	911	3776
33	561	937	3801
150	666	973	3817
154	700	986	3822
155	702	987	3834
320	733	3047	3838
335	740	3607	
368	742	3609	
471	819	3755	

2 SKEINS

310

988

Blanc

TIP:

An embroidery stabiliser provides extra stability and support to the fabric being embroidered. If you choose to use a stabiliser, you will need a 7in (17.8cm) circle for each of the twenty-five blocks. We recommend a wash-away stabiliser, which will leave no trace and not impact the feel or look of the final quilt. You may wish to experiment embroidering both with and without stabiliser to see what you prefer.

FABRIC COLOUR CHART

Use the following colour chart as a guide when choosing the colours of your fabrics. In the Block Layout Guides chapter, all fabrics will be referred to by their chart name, e.g.: 1, 2, X1, X2.

RAINBOW FABRICS

PASTEL FABRICS

Note: X1–X13 may be any pastel shade, they don't have to match those shown here.

You don't have to use just the one rainbow of fabric: you could put together a few rainbows to use repeatedly, or even make a different rainbow for each EPP unit. Follow your creativity! In this case, we recommend laying out all of your embroideries and EPP rings prior to Block Assembly Stage 2: Appliqué EPP Rings, as you may wish to make a different layout that best suits your unique quilt.

Preparing to Begin

This chapter outlines the basic stages for creating Alice's Country Diary Quilt. The good news is, you won't need to use the sewing machine until the very end, when making the quilt, as the construction techniques for the blocks are worked entirely by hand. There's advice, too, for how to get ready to start your sewing journey, from cutting out the paper shapes required for the EPP to preparing your fabrics and threads ready to embroider.

QUILT CONSTRUCTION STAGES

Outlined here are all the stages for making the quilt, for which step-by-step instruction is provided in the chapters that follow. Whether you start the EPP or the embroidery first really doesn't matter, or you could even switch between the two until all the EPP rings and embroidery blocks are complete, before moving on to assemble the blocks. Do whatever works best for you!

EPP TECHNIQUES

Stage 1: Cut out fabric shapes – cutting out the required shapes from the rainbow and pastel fabrics.

Stage 2: Prepare EPP pieces – wrapping the fabric around the paper pieces.

Stage 3: Assemble the rings – stitching the pieces together into a ring.

Stage 4: Remove the papers – removing the papers from the fabric shapes.

EMBROIDERY TECHNIQUES

Stage 1: Transfer the pattern – transferring the pattern onto the background fabric using either the iron-on transfers provided at the back of the book or downloadable trace-on patterns.

Stage 2: Prepare the hoop – putting the embroidery fabric in the hoop.

Stage 3: Embroider the designs – enjoy your slow stitching!

BLOCK ASSEMBLY

Stage 1: Appliqué embroidery – appliquéing the completed embroidery onto the background fabric squares.

Stage 2: Appliqué EPP rings – appliquéing the full EPP rings onto the appliquéd embroideries and appliquéing the half EPP rings onto the background fabric right-angle triangles.

MAKING THE QUILT

Stage 1: Make the quilt top – sewing the completed blocks together to make the quilt top.

Stage 2: Make a quilt sandwich and quilt – layering the quilt layers and holding them together with hand or machine quilting.

Stage 3: Bind the quilt – finishing the edges neatly.

ENGLISH PAPER PIECING (EPP) TEMPLATES

There are four different paper shapes required for the EPP in this quilt, and the templates for these are provided below. How to use the EPP papers to cut out your fabric shapes is explained in detail in the EPP Techniques chapter. Trace off these templates onto card ready to use them to cut out your EPP paper shapes.

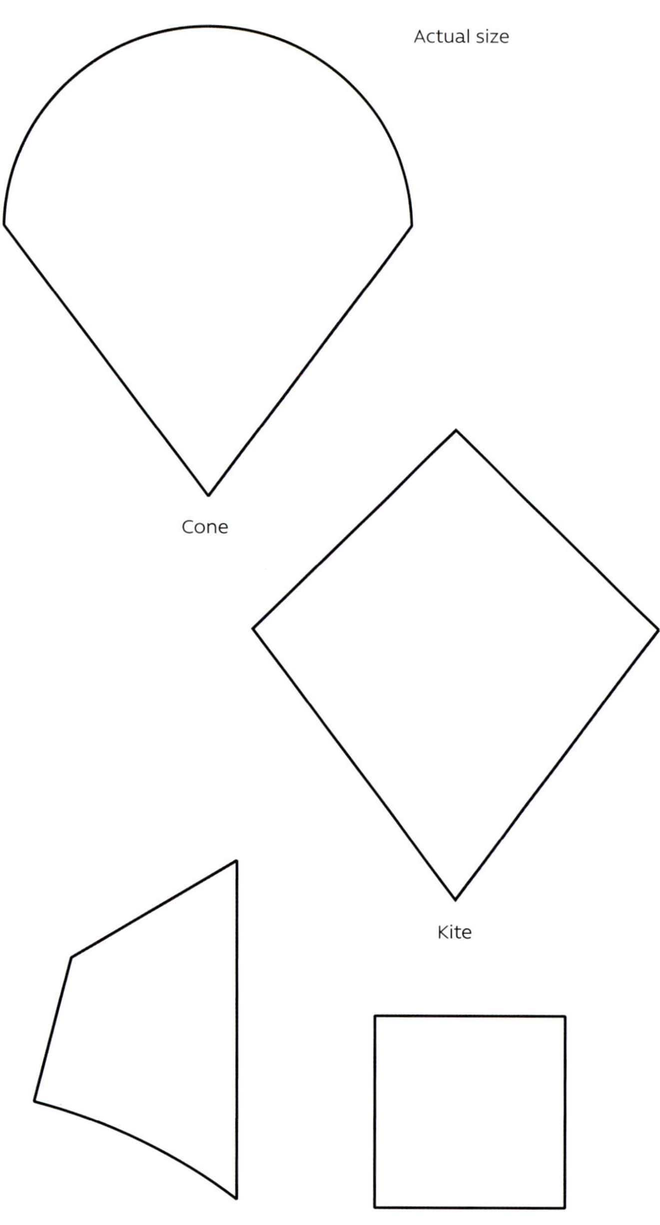

THE ASYMMETRIC TEMPLATE

When laying out the asymmetric shape onto your fabrics, pay careful attention to its orientation as outlined in the Fabric Cutting Lists, as a specific number must be placed with the straight side facing both to the left and to the right. This diagram illustrates how the shapes can be laid out to make the most of your fabric. Note that the red lines on this diagram indicate the ¼in (0.6cm) seam allowance that needs to be allowed for around the paper pieces as you cut out your shapes.

FABRIC CUTTING LISTS

RAINBOW FABRIC 1
- Ten kite shapes
- Eighteen square shapes

RAINBOW FABRIC 2
- Sixteen cone shapes
- Three kite shapes
- Nine square shapes

RAINBOW FABRIC 3
- Ten kite shapes
- Nineteen square shapes

RAINBOW FABRIC 4
- Sixteen cone shapes
- Four kite shapes
- Ten square shapes

RAINBOW FABRIC 5
- Eleven kite shapes
- Eighteen square shapes

RAINBOW FABRIC 6
- Sixteen cone shapes
- Three kite shapes
- Eleven square shapes

RAINBOW FABRIC 7
- Eleven kite shapes
- Eighteen square shapes

RAINBOW FABRIC 8
- Sixteen cone shapes
- Four kite shapes
- Ten square shapes

RAINBOW FABRIC 9
- Ten kite shapes
- Nineteen square shapes

RAINBOW FABRIC 10
- Sixteen cone shapes
- Four kite shapes
- Nine square shapes

RAINBOW FABRIC 11
- Ten kite shapes
- Nineteen square shapes

RAINBOW FABRIC 12
- Sixteen cone shapes
- Three kite shapes
- Ten square shapes

RAINBOW FABRIC 13
- Eleven kite shapes
- Seventeen square shapes

RAINBOW FABRIC 14
- Sixteen cone shapes
- One kite shape
- Eleven square shapes

RAINBOW FABRIC 15
- Eleven kite shapes
- Sixteen square shapes

RAINBOW FABRIC 16
- Sixteen cone shapes
- Two kite shapes
- Ten square shapes

PASTEL FABRICS X1, X3–X9, AND X11–X13

- Nineteen asymmetric shapes, left-facing
- Nineteen asymmetric shapes, right-facing

PASTEL FABRIC X2

- Sixteen asymmetric shapes, left-facing
- Sixteen asymmetric shapes, right-facing

PASTEL FABRIC X10

- Eleven asymmetric shapes, left-facing
- Eleven asymmetric shapes, right-facing

BACKGROUND FABRIC

- Twenty-five 13in (33cm) squares for the block assembly
- Twenty-five circles approximately 11½–12in (29.2–30.5cm) in diameter for the embroideries
- Six 12½in (31.75cm) squares, then sub-cut into twelve right-angled triangles for the block assembly
- One 12½in (31.75cm) square, then sub-cut on both diagonals to give you four corner setting triangles for making the quilt top

TIP:

When cutting the same layout of asymmetric shapes for some of the pastel fabrics, you can layer up to four fabrics on top of each other and multi cut. After stacking, pin one set of paper shapes through all layers. Cut out the shapes using a rotary cutter and mat only, as cutting multiple layers accurately with scissors is far more difficult. Once cut, separate the cut fabric pieces and attach a paper shape to each.

TIP:

The background fabric circles are cut much larger than required so if the circle isn't perfect or the selvedge is included at the edges that's perfectly fine. These circles will be cut down to their finished size of 7in (17.8cm) after the embroidery is complete, as will be explained in step-by-step detail in Block Assembly.

FABRIC PREPARATION

While it should not be necessary to pre-wash Liberty Tana Lawn® in particular, you may do so if you wish. For any other fabric we do recommend that you pre-wash prior to cutting. Place the fabric in a delicates bag and wash with like colours at no more than 30°C (86°F) using a gentle wash cycle and mild detergent. A zig-zag stitch around the edges of the fabric will help to prevent fraying while it is in the wash; however, if the wash is gentle enough, this may not be necessary. Line dry in the shade, then use a hot iron with steam to press flat.

EPP Techniques

English Paper Piecing (EPP) is an easy hand-sewing technique which involves small pieces of fabric being wrapped around paper before being sewn together. The paper provides stability when sewing and helps ensure the shape of the piece is accurate. This chapter provides step-by-step instruction for creating the EPP full ring and half ring designs seen on Alice's Country Diary Quilt.

STAGE 1: CUT OUT FABRIC SHAPES

1. First, press all your fabrics flat. Then, referring to the information provided in the Fabric Cutting Lists (see Preparing to Begin), lay out the exact number and type of pre-cut paper shapes required onto the indicated fabrics, wrong side of fabric facing up. Secure each pre-cut paper shape in place using either a dab of soluble glue (our preferred method) or a small-headed pin. Be sure to leave a ¼in (0.6cm) gap around the outside of each of the paper shapes as this will be your seam allowance.

2. Cut around each shape, being sure to include the ¼in (0.6cm) seam allowance on each. (Note: if you are using acrylic templates, cut exactly around the template.) We recommend using a rotary cutter and mat to cut out your shapes; however, it may also be completed using scissors.

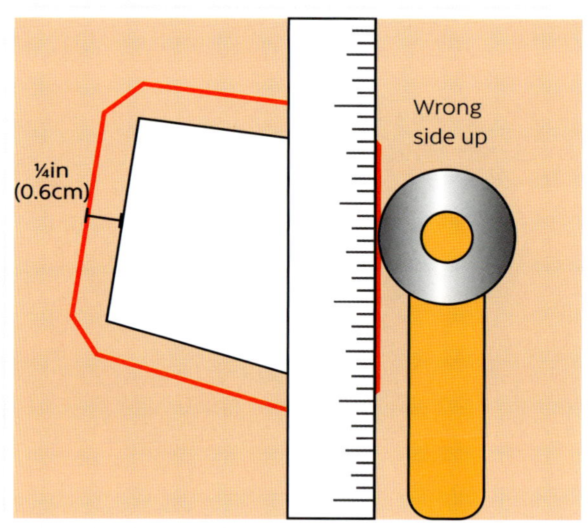

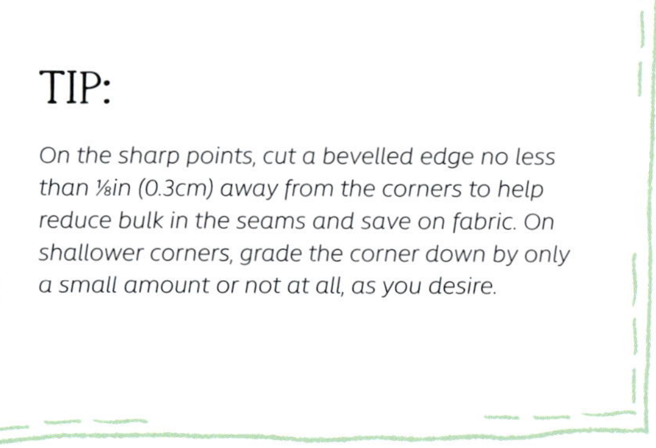

TIP:

On the sharp points, cut a bevelled edge no less than ⅛in (0.3cm) away from the corners to help reduce bulk in the seams and save on fabric. On shallower corners, grade the corner down by only a small amount or not at all, as you desire.

STAGE 2: PREPARE EPP PIECES

KITE, SQUARE AND ASYMMETRIC TEMPLATES

For these shapes, use one of the following methods to wrap the fabric around the paper shapes.

Glue Basting

This is our preferred method. Place the paper shape on the wrong side of the cut fabric shape, leaving the ¼in (0.6cm) seam allowance of fabric around all the edges of the paper shape. Using a glue pen, glue along one edge of the paper and carefully fold the fabric over the edge, lightly pressing it in place. Repeat for all sides of the shape, working in a single direction until the paper shape is wrapped by the fabric on all sides.

Thread Basting

Place the paper shape on the wrong side of the cut fabric shape, leaving ¼in (0.6cm) seam allowance of fabric all around. Fold one edge of the fabric over the paper shape, and, starting with a knot, tack (baste) in place through fabric and paper, using stitches approximately ⅜in (1cm) long. Repeat for all sides of the shape, working in a single direction until the paper is wrapped by the fabric on all sides, finishing with a knot. There is no need to be neat as these stitches will be removed later, but make sure there is a stitch at each corner to hold the folded fabric in place.

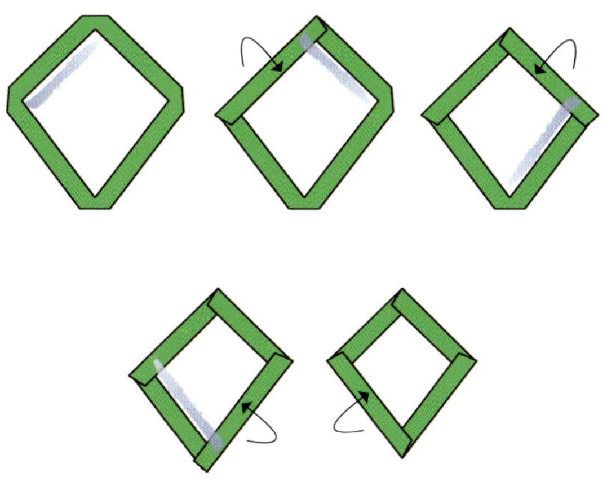

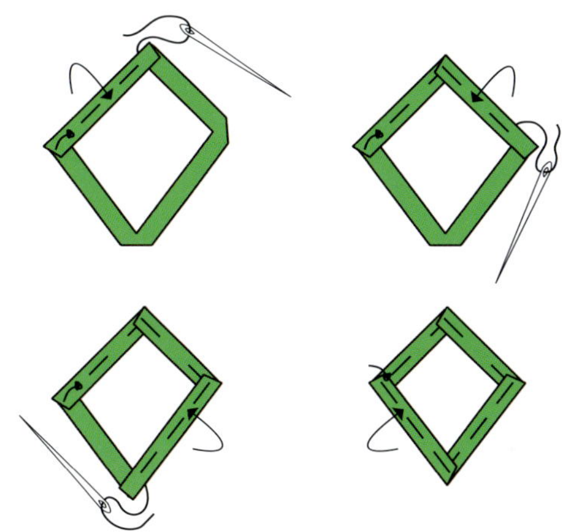

TIP:

EPP is really mobile – take it on holiday, to appointment waiting rooms, or even your local sewing group. Store your pieces in a clean pouch or cosmetic bag large enough to hold your fabric, papers, glue pen, needle, small scissors, thimble and thread.

CONE TEMPLATE

For this shape, use one of the following methods to wrap the fabric around the paper shapes.

Glue and Thread Basting

This is our preferred method. Place the paper shape on the wrong side of the cut fabric shape, leaving the ¼in (0.6cm) seam allowance of fabric around all the edges of the paper shape. Using a glue pen, glue along one straight edge of the paper and carefully fold the fabric over the edge, lightly pressing it in place. Repeat for the remaining straight side of the paper shape.

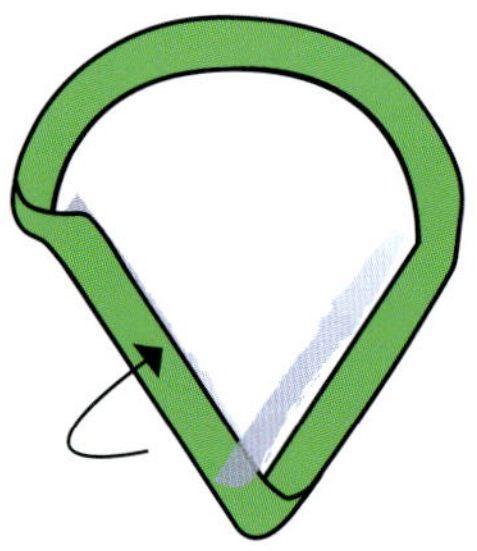

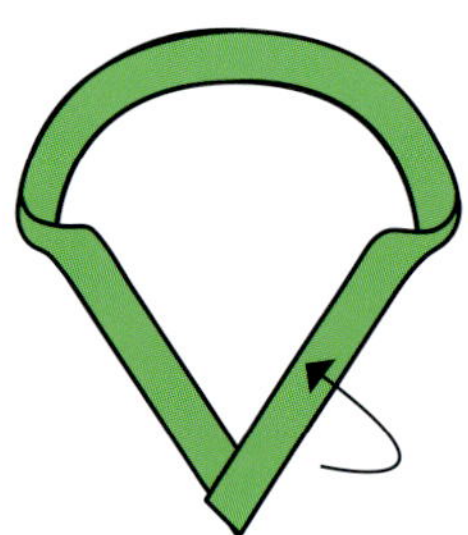

Thread a hand sewing needle and make a knot at one end. Sew an even running stitch along the fabric of the curve, then gently pull on the thread to gather the fabric; make a knot close to the fabric to secure once you are happy with how the fabric is gathered.

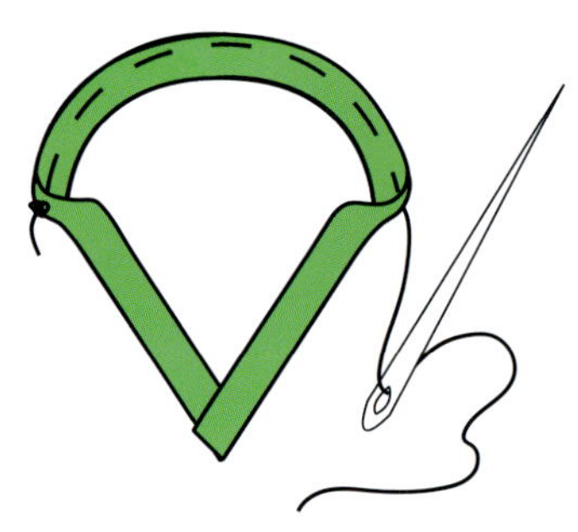

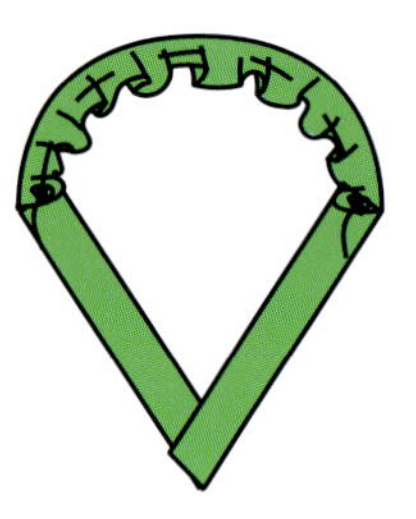

Thread Basting

Place the paper shape on the wrong side of the cut fabric shape, allowing a ¼in (0.6cm) seam allowance all around. Thread a hand sewing needle and make a knot at one end. Fold the fabric around one straight edge of the paper. Tack (baste) in place through fabric and paper, using stitches approximately ⅜in (1cm) long and repeat to continue along the other straight side, ensuring there is a stitch near the corner to hold the folded fabric in place.

Using the same length of thread, sew an even running stitch along the fabric of the curve, then gently pull on the thread to gather the fabric; make a knot close to the fabric to secure once you are happy with how the fabric is gathered.

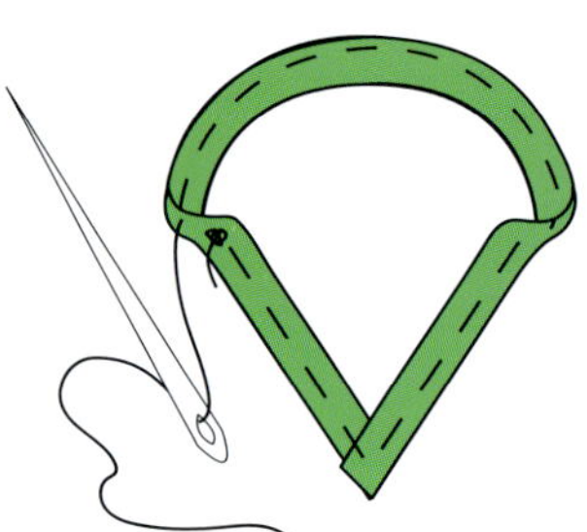

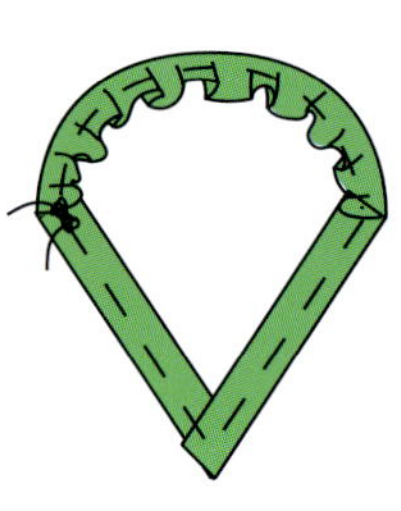

TIP:

Completing all the gluing or thread basting for a ring or project in one go is handy as you can then take the fully prepared shapes out and about and sew where you wish. EPP is so versatile and can be sewn anywhere!

STAGE 3: ASSEMBLE THE RINGS

Before sewing the prepared EPP fabric shapes together to form the full and half rings required for the quilt blocks as seen in the Block Layout Guides chapter, please pay attention to the following notes.

For all shapes that sit along the inner edge of the ring (coloured pink in the diagrams below), be sure to carefully align the shapes at the points where they meet the inner ring's edge (shown in green). Aligning these points accurately first will result in a better ring shape.

When sewing these same shapes (i.e. those that meet the inner ring's edge), always sew from the centre outwards, as indicated by the green and red arrows in the diagrams below. This keeps the tension across the EPP ring even.

1. Take two adjacent shapes and place them alongside each other, right sides facing up, aligning the straight edge to be joined, just as they appear in the block layout guide (referring to the Block Layout Guides chapter). Flip one shape over the other (so right sides are together) maintaining the necessary alignment. Quilt clips can be really useful for keeping the shapes in position when sewing.

2. Thread a hand sewing needle and run the thread through your fingers two or three times to reduce twisting (use a thread conditioner, if you wish).

3. Stitch the shapes together along the edge to be joined, working a whipstitch through the edge of the fabric only, as follows: take the needle in on one side, out the other and back around to the side you started on to push it in again. Make stitches as close together as you can, picking up just a few threads of each fabric shape with the needle as you stitch. This makes the seams strong and the stitches almost invisible. (Knot the thread at the start only, and continue to use the same length of thread for the next shape to be added, continuing until it runs out, when you should knot to finish.)

4. Open out the joined shapes. Take another shape adjacent to those already sewn together and whipstitch together in the same way. Continue in this way until the full or half ring is formed as seen in the block layout guide. Don't hesitate to fold the work-in-progress EPP ring in different ways in order to make it easier to sew the edges together – any creases can be pressed out with an iron after assembly.

5. Once the full or half ring is complete, press it flat using starch to help it keep its shape.

TIP:

It is a good idea to anchor the thread to the needle to stop the thread from pulling through. First, tie a knot at the bottom of the thread as usual. Then simply tie a knot with the other end of the thread around the eye of the needle. This keeps the thread more securely attached to the needle and avoids the need for endless rethreading.

STAGE 4: REMOVE THE PAPERS

1. Once the EPP full and half rings have been assembled, all papers must be removed from the finished units. If glue basted: dab the folded-down seam allowances with a little water, to help release the fabric from the paper. If thread basted: snip the thread away taking care not to snip the fabric, then take the papers out.

2. Press the completed EPP rings flat, being careful to keep all seam allowances still folded back underneath the shapes at the edges. Pay special attention to any curved edges - spray starch can help with this. If the seam allowances on thin, pointy sections overhang the front of the completed EPP rings, don't worry; they will be hidden once the ring is sewn onto the background quilt fabric.

3. Store the completed EPP pieces somewhere safe, flat and out of direct sunlight, until you are ready to appliqué them onto the background fabric to complete the quilt blocks.

TIP:

If undamaged, removed papers may be used again; simply iron them without steam to make them crisp and flat once more.

Embroidery Techniques

This chapter includes all the technique information you'll need to work the twenty-five embroideries featured in The Embroideries chapter with confidence, including an introduction to each of the stitches used, and tips on starting and finishing your stitching. If you are new to embroidery, the stitch sampler is a very good place to begin, and an iron-on transfer has been included for this too.

STRAIGHT STITCH

This stitch will create short lines, an essential stitch when adding details to insects and flowers.

TO MAKE THIS STITCH

Bring the needle up at point A, then down at your desired stitch length at point B.

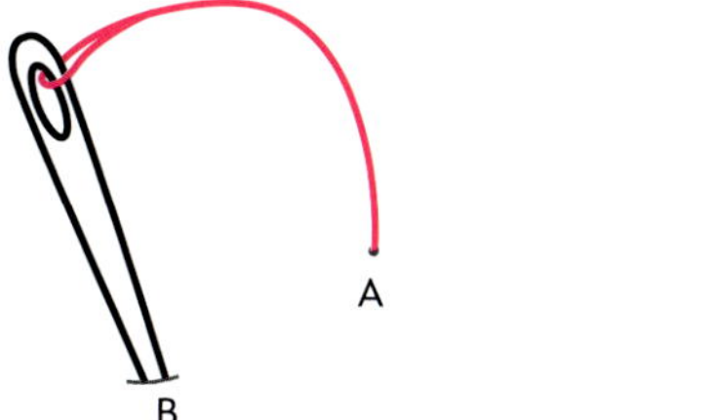

SATIN STITCH

This stitch involves lots of straight stitches close together to fill an area. For best results, ensure that stitches are parallel – the threads should lay flat and not be twisted. Don't pull the stitches too tight to avoid fabric puckering, and always stitch to the outside edge of a traced line.

TO MAKE THIS STITCH

Starting in the middle of the shape to be filled, bring the needle up at point A and down at point B, directly opposite, then back up again at C, next to point A. Continue in this way to fill one half, then fill the other half in the same way.

To fill a leaf shape: Mark the central line of the leaf on the fabric. Bring the needle up at point A (at the centre top), then down at point B (about a third of the way down the length of the leaf), and back up again at point C next to point A. Space the stitches on the outside edge slightly wider apart and those on the central line much closer together, to account for the curve. Continue in this way to fill one half of the leaf, then fill the other half in the same way.

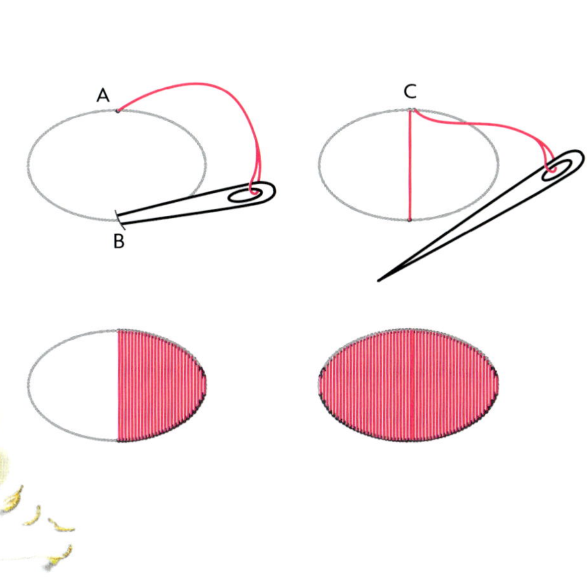

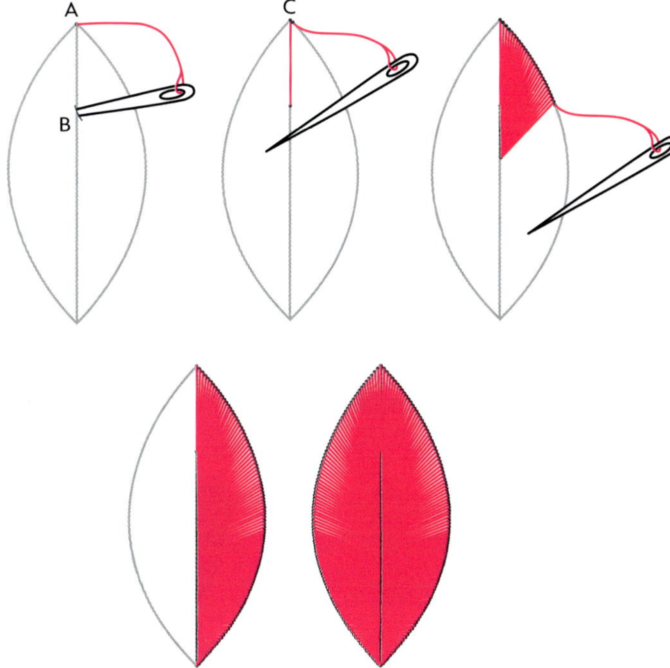

BACK STITCH

This stitch creates a solid line from multiple straight stitches. It can also be used to fill an area.

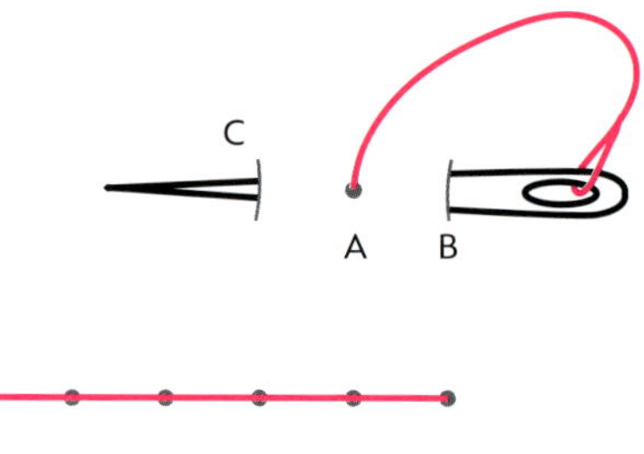

TO MAKE THIS STITCH

Bring the needle up at point A, then take the needle backwards and down at point B and bring it up again at point C. Take the needle backwards again, down at point A and up again a stitch length in front. Repeat, so that each new stitch is made with a backwards motion. Keep the length of the stitches even, ensuring that they join in a continuous line.

SPLIT BACK STITCH

This stitch creates a line that is a little jagged, or even a bit fluffy in appearance. It can be worked as a single line, or as multiple rows together to fill a shape for subtle shading. The length of the stitches can be as small or long as you like depending on the effect you want to achieve.

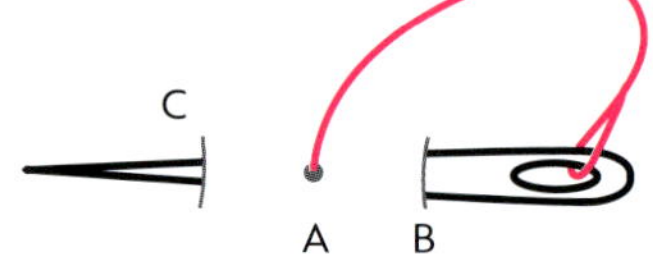

TO MAKE THIS STITCH

Bring the needle up at point A, then take the needle backwards and down at point B and bring it up again at point C. Taking the needle backwards again, bring it down at point D, directly through the thread of the previous stitch, and up again at point E in front of the stitch just made. Continue in this way, keeping the length of the stitches even, until the row is formed as desired. To finish, bring the needle down directly through the previous stitch.

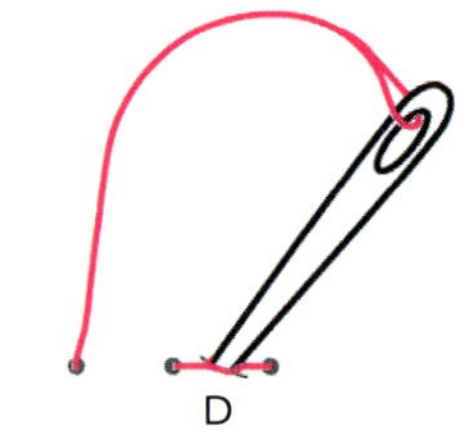

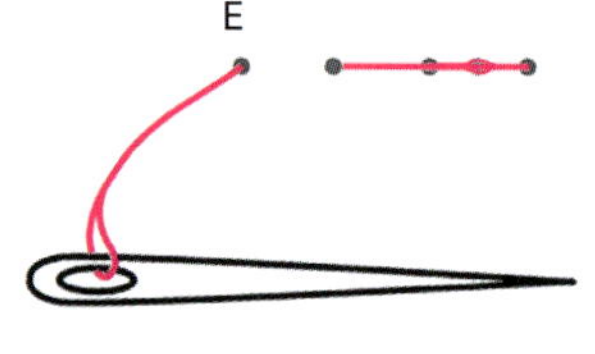

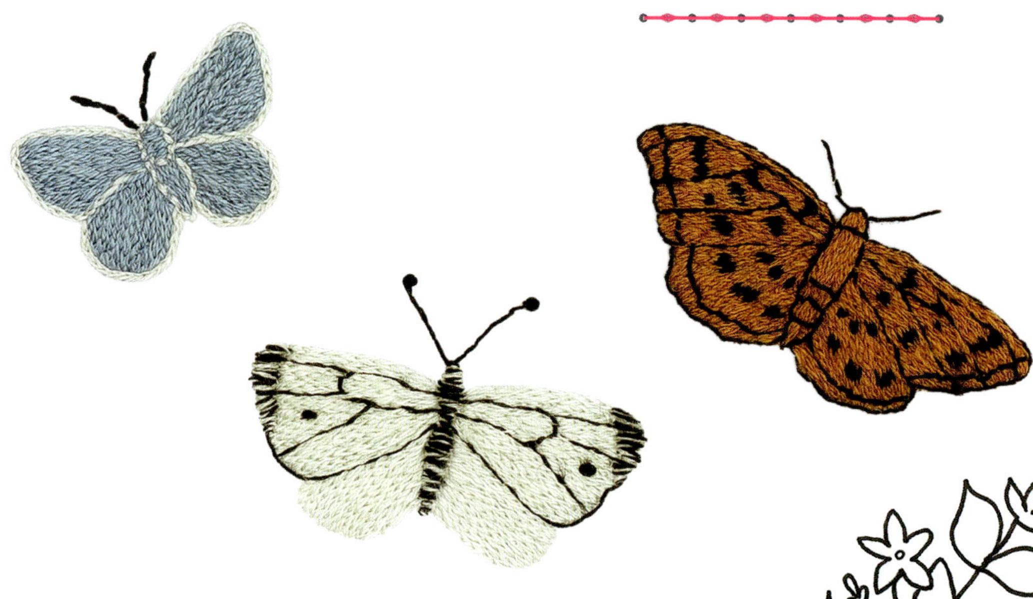

LONG AND SHORT STITCH

This stitch is especially useful for filling fan-shaped areas, such as petals. Rows of alternating long and short stitches work together to create gradual curves. For best results, don't pull the stitches too tight to avoid fabric puckering, and make sure the threads are not twisted. Angle the stitches slightly to suit the shapes being filled and always stitch to the outside edge of a traced line.

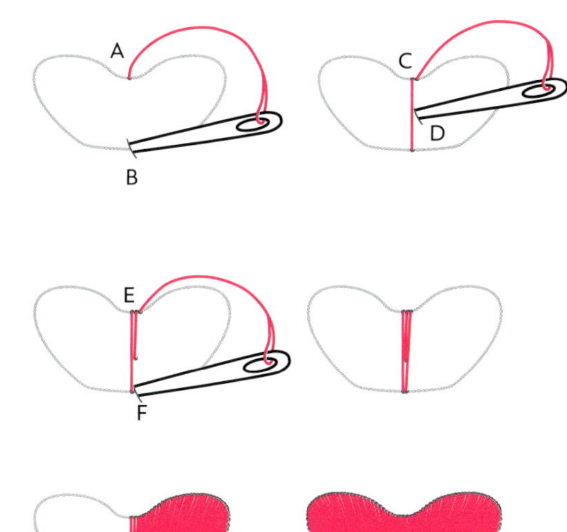

TO MAKE THIS STITCH

Starting in the middle of the shape to be filled, bring the needle up at point A, then down at point B to make a long stitch. Bring the needle back up at point C directly next to point A, then down at point D, just over half the length of the first stitch. Adjust the length of the short stitch according to what looks best to fill the shape. Bring the needle up at point E directly next to point C, then down at point F directly next to point B. Continue in this way to fill half the shape. Then fill the remaining half of the shape in the same way.

TIP:

When practising your embroidery stitches, aim to keep your stitches even by pulling each stitch with the same amount of tension. A too loose stitch will look floppy and a too tight stitch will pucker the fabric.

FRENCH KNOT

This stitch makes a raised, round dot. These stitches are easily crushed so it's best to leave them until last. The finished size of the knot may be adjusted by changing the number of times the thread is wrapped around the needle and the thickness of the thread (i.e. the number of strands used in the needle).

TO MAKE THIS STITCH

Bring the needle up at point A and hold the thread firmly with your fingers 1½in (3.8cm) away from the fabric. Wrap the thread over the needle shaft (wrapping twice is fairly standard but do adjust depending on your desired outcome). Keeping the thread taut, take the needle back down at point B (very close to point A). With the thread still taut, pull the needle through the fabric and just as the eye of the needle passes through the fabric, place your thumb over the wrapped thread to hold it in place. Continue pulling the thread through until the loose thread disappears under your thumb and the knot sits securely on the fabric's surface.

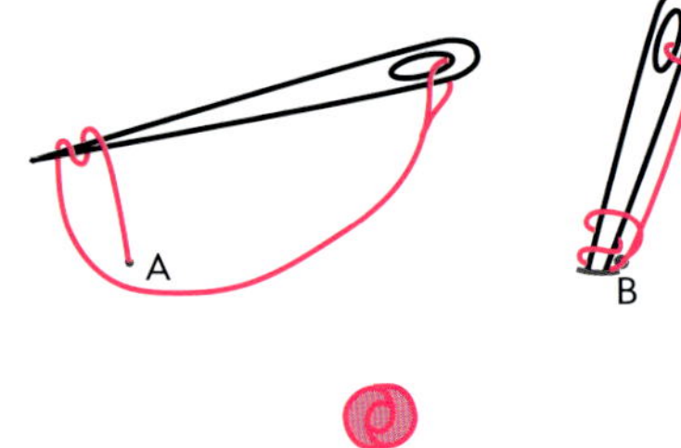

LAZY DAISY STITCH

This stitch creates a small petal or leaf shape, which can be used as single stitches or grouped together.

TO MAKE THIS STITCH

Bring the needle up at point A, then down at point B, directly next to point A, leaving the thread loose, and bring the needle up again at point C, a short distance opposite, positioning the needle over the thread. Pull the needle through completely then take it down at point D (just above point C) to trap the thread in place. To maintain a full petal shape, do not pull the thread too tightly.

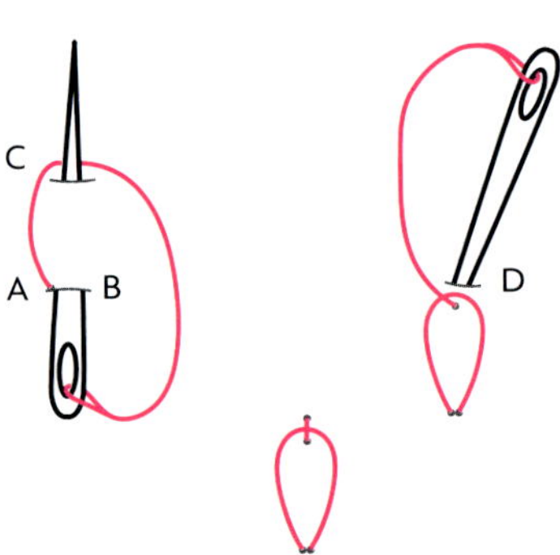

CHAIN STITCH

This stitch creates a row of loop 'chains'. These can be used in lines as well as to outline or fill a shape. Do not pull the thread too tight and keep the size of each loop the same.

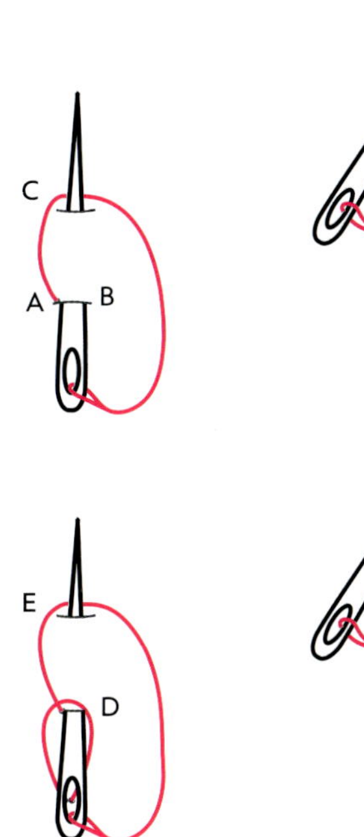

TO MAKE THIS STITCH

Bring the needle up at point A, then down at point B, directly next to point A, leaving the thread loose, and bring the needle up again at point C, a short distance opposite, positioning the needle over the thread. Pull the needle through completely to make your first 'link' in the chain. Now take the needle down again at point D (i.e. directly next to point C), then up again at point E with the needle over the thread. Do not pull the thread too tightly to maintain a full loop. Continue in this way. To secure the chain, at the top of the last loop, make a single short stitch to hold the thread in place.

To use chain stitch to fill a shape: Stitch around the outside working into the middle.

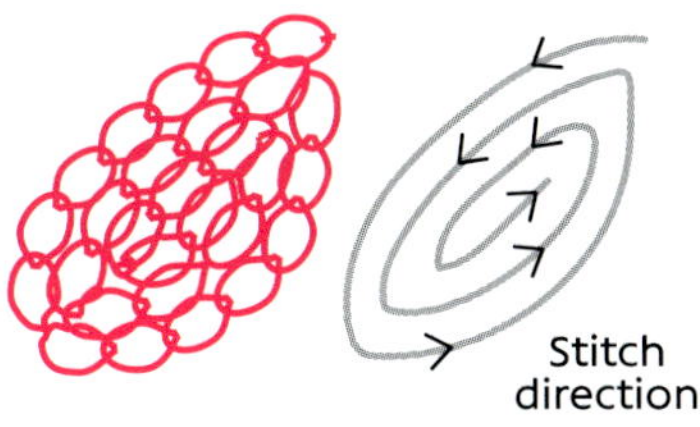

EMBROIDERY TECHNIQUES

COUCHING

This stitch is worked with two threads, with one thread being laid on top of the fabric and a second thread being used to anchor it in place, with small straight stitches worked over the first thread at regular intervals. These threads may be the same or different colours (for clarity, different thread colours have been used in the diagrams). The laid thread may be composed of several strands of thread and is often thicker than the anchoring thread, which is generally just a single thread.

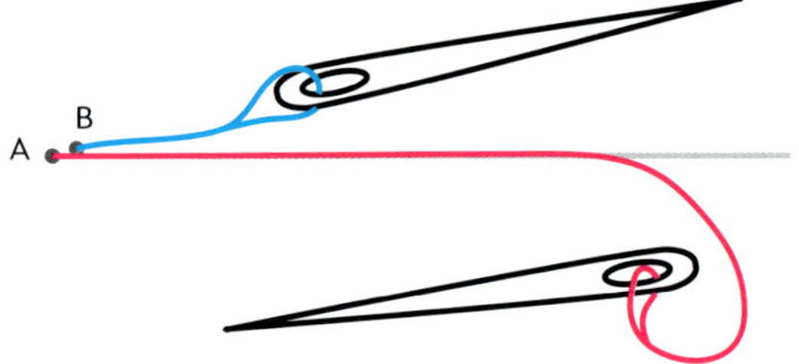

TO MAKE THIS STITCH

Thread two needles with the threads required. Bring the laid thread (shown in pink) up at point A at the very end of the design line. Now bring the anchoring thread (shown in blue) up at point B. Arrange the laid thread to follow the design line on top of the fabric and bring the anchoring thread down over the laid thread at point C, making a small stitch to hold it in place. Bring the thread up again a short distance away to make another anchoring stitch. Continue in this way, along the length of the traced line. To finish, bring both threads to the back of the fabric and knot to secure.

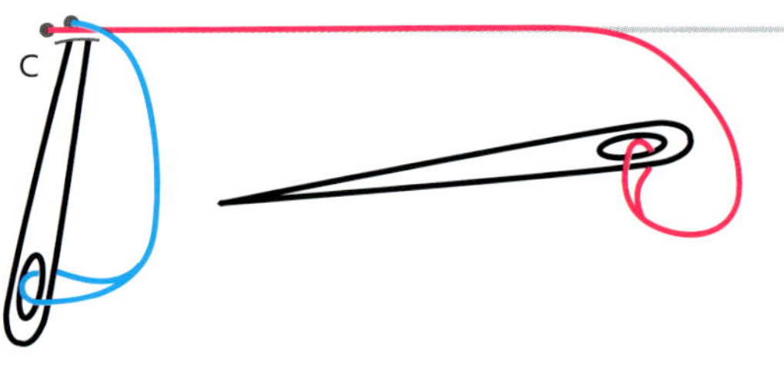

STAGE 1: TRANSFER THE PATTERN

There are a couple of ways that you can transfer the pattern onto your embroidery fabric, either by using the iron-on transfers provided at the back of this book or by using the digital patterns (available for download) to trace the designs directly onto the fabric.

USING IRON-ON TRANSFERS

1. Remove the transfer from the back of the book, tearing carefully along the perforated strip. Trim around the circumference of the design to leave a border of excess paper, trimming off the block identification label.

2. Take a background fabric circle and press it smooth with an iron (do not use steam setting).

3. Place the transfer design ink-side down so it is centrally placed in the fabric circle. With the iron set to its hottest setting (again, no steam), carefully press the iron onto the transfer for about 45 seconds. Keep the iron still so that the ink does not bleed.

4. Remove the iron and carefully peel back a corner of the paper to check the design has transferred successfully. If it hasn't, smooth the paper back down and repeat step 3.

Iron-on transfers are provided for each of the embroideries at the back of the book. Alternatively, you can access the downloadable patterns at www.bookmarkedhub.com. These can also prove useful for alignment accuracy in the block assembly.

USING TRACE-ON PATTERNS

1. Take a background fabric circle and press it smooth with an iron.

2. Print the download pattern and place it right side facing up in front of a light source (either onto a light box if you have one, or by taping it up against a window) to help you to better see the design. Place the fabric circle on top, ensuring it is right side up (if your fabric has a right side). Arrange it so the embroidery pattern is roughly central. The lines of the embroidery pattern should be visible through the fabric.

3. Using an erasable fabric marker pen of your choice, trace all the lines of the embroidery pattern onto the fabric, including the pattern's outer circle line and direction markers. Hold the fabric firm and flat while tracing.

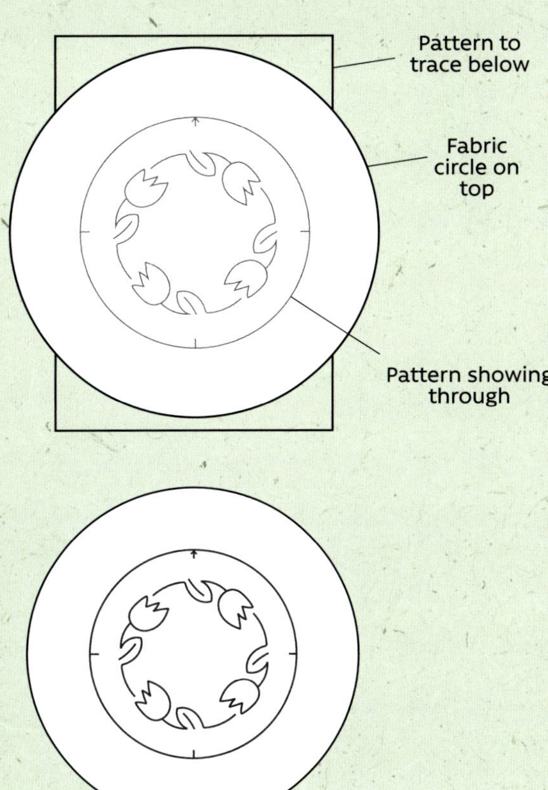

STAGE 2: PREPARE THE HOOP

When placing your embroidery fabric in a hoop, it should be screwed tight enough so that the fabric does not slip.

1. Separate the inner and outer rings of your embroidery hoop. Place the inner hoop on a flat surface. Place the fabric circle on top with the transferred pattern facing up, centring it within the hoop.

2. Fit the outer hoop over the inner ring, sandwiching the fabric between. Tighten the screw so the fabric is held gently.

3. The fabric must be even and taut in the hoop, but not distorted. To achieve this, pull evenly on the fabric around the whole circumference. It should be firm and without any give when tapped on, just like a drum.

4. Once this has been achieved, tighten the screw until it won't tighten any more. If the screw is difficult to tighten, use a small screwdriver or pair of pliers.

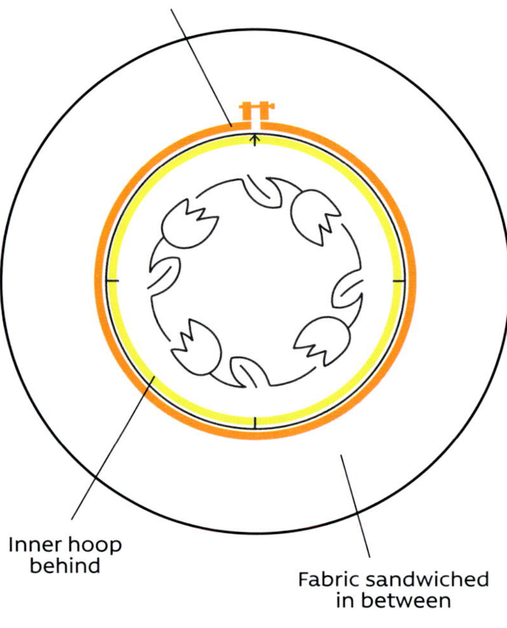

TIP:

The excess fabric around the ring may become dirty and fray due to regular handling while embroidering. This is completely normal so don't worry. The background fabric circle has been cut deliberately larger than the necessary finished size to account for this and it will be cut down at the block assembly stage.

STAGE 3: EMBROIDER THE DESIGNS

The details of working the embroideries are included in The Embroideries chapter. However, everything you need to know to start and finish your stitching is included here.

STARTING STITCHING

Referring to The Embroideries chapter for the number of strands and thread colour to use for each element of the design, prepare your thread and needle for embroidery.

To help conserve thread, as well as make threading the needle and the overall handling of the threads easier, odd and even numbers of strands are treated differently.

Cutting the Thread

For odd numbers of strands: Cut a length of thread no more than 24in (61cm), approximately an arm's length, from the skein of embroidery thread. Any longer and it becomes unwieldy, any shorter and you may feel like you are having to rethread too often.

For even numbers of strands: Cut a length of thread no more than 35in (89cm), approximately hand to opposite shoulder length, from the skein of embroidery thread. These threads will be only half this length once threaded and knotted on the needle.

Pulling the Strands

Once the appropriate length of thread has been cut, pull a single strand of thread out at a time from the cut length until you have the number of strands needed.

For odd numbers of strands: Pull the exact number required; so if, for example, three strands are required, pull three strands of thread.

For even numbers of strands: Pull only half of the required strands as you will use them doubled over; so if, for example, four strands are required, pull only two strands of thread.

Arrange all of the pulled strands together, aligning their ends neatly.

Threading the Needle

For odd numbers of strands: Thread all of the strands through the eye of the needle, using a needle threader if required. Make a knot at just one end (see To Knot the Thread), leaving the other end of the thread loose.

For even numbers of strands: Arrange the strands so that there is an even amount of thread on either side of the needle, then bring both ends together and knot all threads at once (see To Knot the Thread).

TIP:

If the thread becomes tangled as you embroider, simply drop the threaded needle and let it hang freely until it unwinds itself. Repeat as many times as necessary.

TO KNOT THE THREAD

Place the end of the thread you wish to knot at the tip of the needle, with the needle on top and the thread end extending about ¼in (0.6cm) beyond the needle.

Wrap the long end of the thread over and around the needle's shaft twice, close together. For a larger knot, wrap it more times.

Pinch the wrapped thread to hold it in place while pulling the needle away as far as it will go. Still pinching, slide the wrapped thread along the length of the needle and continuing down the length of the thread, finally settling at the end as a knot.

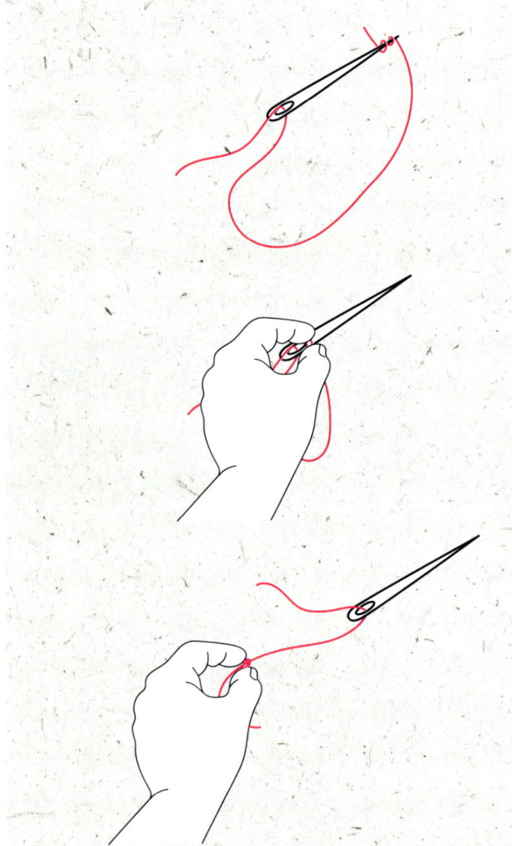

Inserting the Needle

Push the needle through from the back of the fabric to the front, and pull the thread through until the knot is against the back of the fabric. Tug gently on the thread to check it does not come through the fabric to the front. If it does, simply make a larger knot and start again!

TIP:

When working the embroidery, you should be able to pull the needle and thread through the fabric without much trouble. If the thread makes a loud 'zipper' sound, or there is significant resistance, you probably need to change up to a bigger size needle (e.g. if using a 10, change to a 9). A larger needle will make a larger hole, meaning the thread comes through more easily. However, the hole the needle makes should be just enough for the thread to pass through - a visible hole should not be left around the thread.

FINISHING STITCHING

Finishing a Thread

To finish a length of thread when stitching, choose from the following methods. An unobtrusive finish such as that described in method 1 is especially good if you will continue stitching in the same area as lots of bulkier knots can get in the way of your stitching.

Method 1: Bring the needle through to the back of the fabric and pass it tightly back and forth through the stitches already made. Once the thread is secured, snip off the end.

Method 2: Bring the needle through to the back of the fabric and knot close to the fabric to secure. Snip the thread end close to the knot.

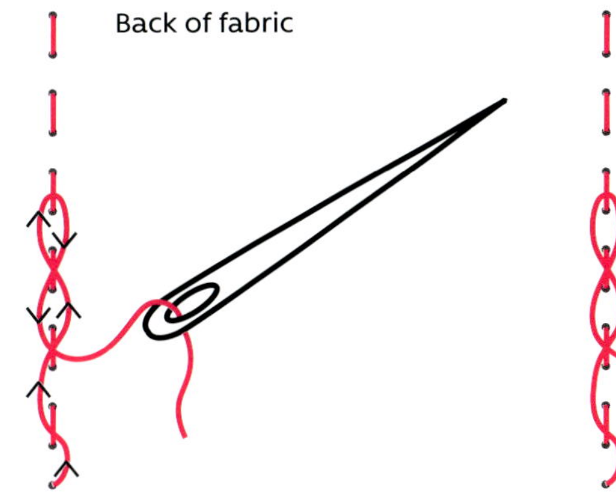

Finishing a thread, method 1.

Completing the Embroidery

When the whole of the embroidery of the design is complete, remove it from the hoop. If you have used the downloaded trace-on patterns rather than the transfers provided at the back of the book, then follow the manufacturer's instructions to remove any visible traced marks from the embroidered design only (i.e. leaving the traced outside circle marks in place).

Iron the embroidery from the back to remove any wrinkles that have formed when stitching but take care over any areas of textural stitching (e.g. French knots) as they may become misshapen; this can be prevented by placing a thick, soft towel under the project as you iron.

Store the completed embroideries somewhere safe, flat and out of direct sunlight, until you are ready to appliqué them onto the EPP rings.

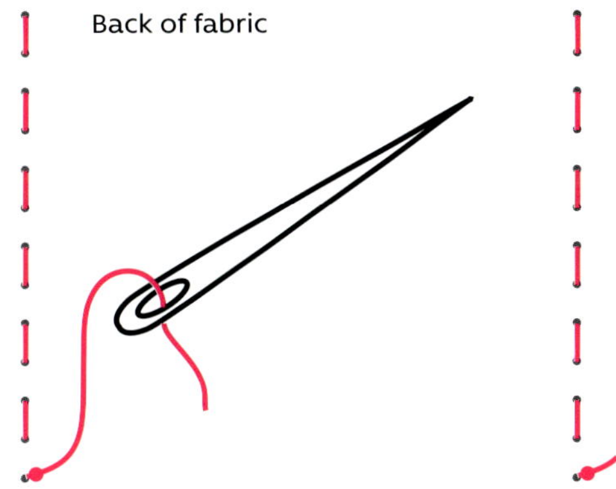

Finishing a thread, method 2.

TIP:

Always start and stop embroidering within the same section. Secure the thread and cut it off, then move on to a new place to start by securing the thread to stitch again. Do not be tempted to leave a long trail of thread between same colour sections, as these threads are in danger of being visible from the front of the design, impacting its appearance.

Block Assembly

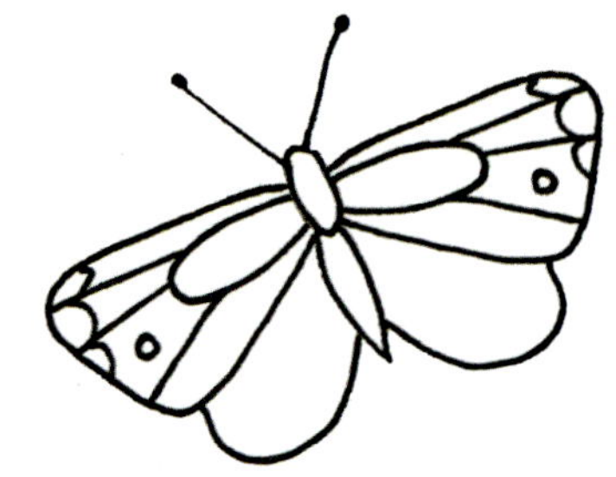

Once you have finished the EPP and the embroideries, it's time to attach them to the background fabric squares or triangles to make the full ring and half ring blocks required to complete the quilt. As you do so, you'll need to refer to the Block Layout Guides chapter, which includes diagrams of each of the blocks in the context of the finished quilt.

STAGE 1: APPLIQUÉ EMBROIDERY

1. Take one of the 13 x 13in (33 x 33cm) background fabric squares and press it flat.

2. Find the centre of the square by folding it in half, then in half again, creasing each fold line well. Unfold.

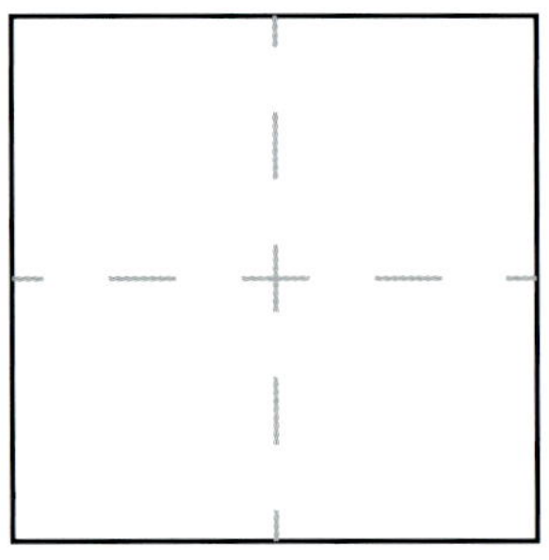

3. Now fold in half diagonally, first one way and then the other, creasing well, then unfold. This diagonal line indicates the up and down direction of the block. Orientate the fabric square as shown in the diagram below.

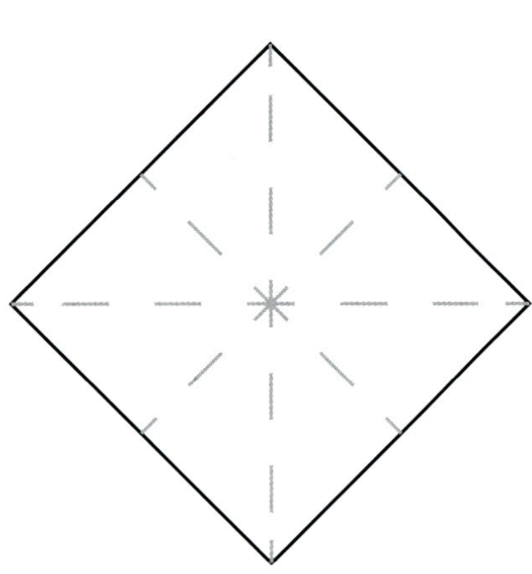

4. Trace off or download and print out the circle template (see Circle Template), then cut it out. Using a light source (either a light box or a window), lay the completed embroidery circle over the circle template. Making sure that the embroidery design is the right way up and centred within the inner circle, trace around the outer circle. If you have used downloaded trace-on patterns for the embroidery designs (see Embroidery Techniques: Transfer the Pattern), the direction markers of the embroidery design that help you to align the embroidery circle on the background square are already in place and you may only need to refresh them. If you have used the iron-on transfers included in this book, then use an erasable fabric marker to trace the inner circle. Also mark the north, south, east and west directional markers (it's best to do this within the seam allowance – i.e. the ½in/1.3cm space between the outer and inner circle – if possible). Use fabric scissors to cut out neatly around the outer circle and discard the excess fabric.

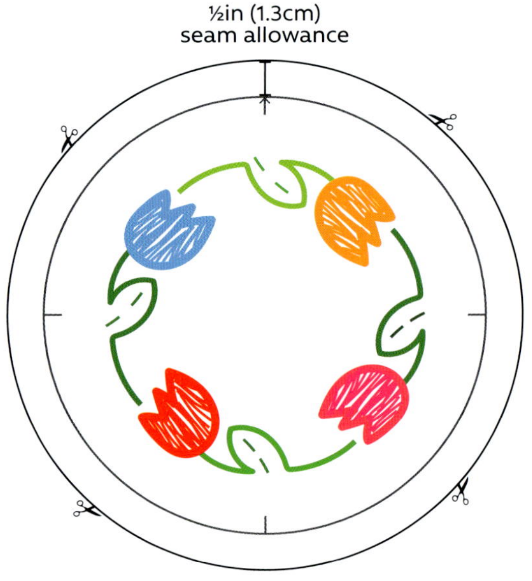

5. Place the trimmed embroidery circle right side up on top of the on-point fabric square, arranging it so that the directional markers of the embroidery circle are aligned with the upwards crease on the background fabric. Make sure the embroidery circle is flat and, once you are happy with the placement, pin it in place.

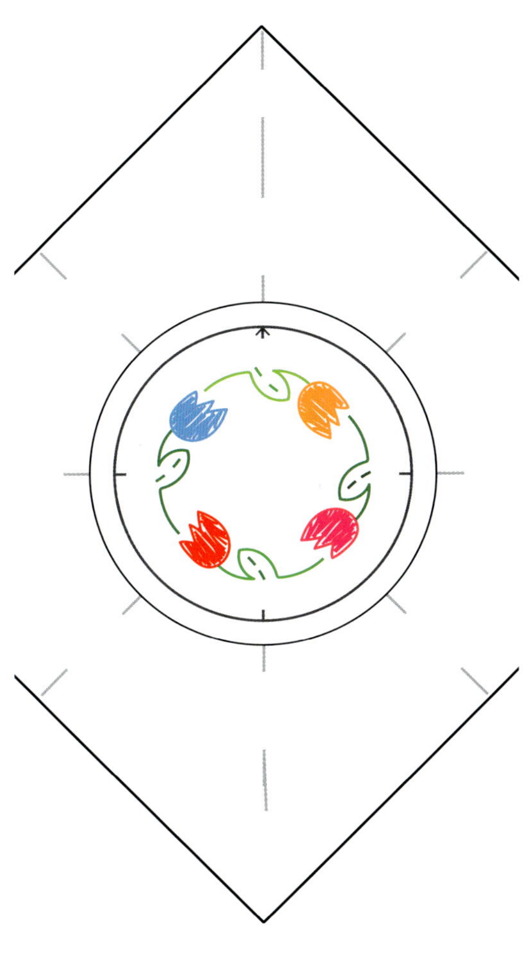

6. Thread a hand sewing needle with thread matching the background fabric colour and tie a knot at one end of the thread. Insert the needle from the back of the background fabric square, close to the embroidery circle fabric. Tug on the thread to check it does not come through the fabric to the front. If it does, simply make a larger knot in the thread and start again. Stitch the embroidery circle to the background fabric using tacking (basting) stitches about ½–1in (1.3-2.6cm) long around the circle's seam allowance only. Do not stitch within the traced inner circle (which marks the boundary of the embroidery design on the block). Be sure to keep the embroidery circle fabric flat as you stitch. Finish by knotting on the reverse side. Remove pins.

STAGE 2: APPLIQUÉ EPP RINGS

When appliquéing the full EPP rings to the prepared background squares from Stage 1, refer to the block layout guides (see Block Layout Guides) for which type of ring – cone shape or kite shape – to attach to the block you are working on.

FOR FULL EPP RING

1. Take a full EPP ring and a prepared background fabric square (i.e. with the embroidery circle tacked (basted) in place). Arrange the EPP ring flat on top of the background fabric, right side up, so that the outer points (red dots) of the cone or kite shapes align with the creases of the fabric square and the inner edge of the EPP ring aligns with the drawn or traced inner circle on the embroidery. The correct alignment of the EPP ring is very important to keep the intended shape. Once you are happy with the ring placement, pin or tack in place.

Cone Shape Alignment

Kite Shape Alignment

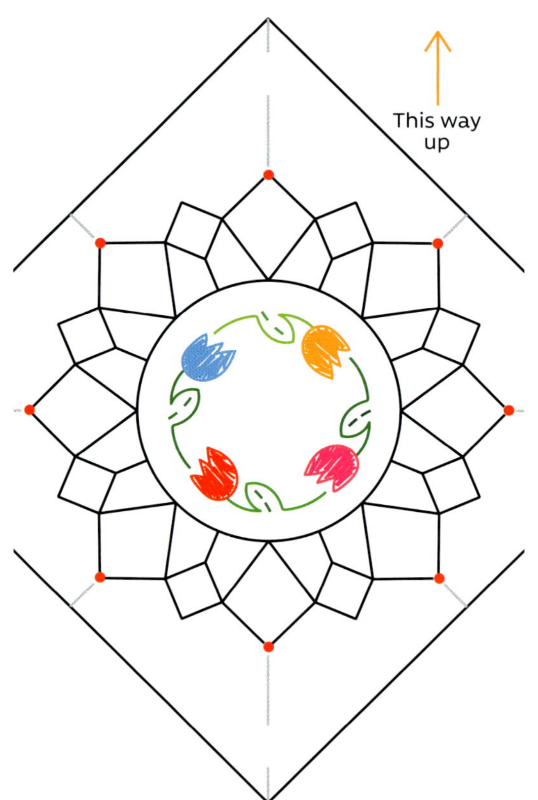

2. Use blind stitch to appliqué the EPP ring in place around the outside and inside edges of the ring as indicated by the red lines in the diagrams (see Blind Stitch Appliqué Method).

3. Evenly trim the block down to 12½ x 12½in (31.75 x 31.75cm). Store the completed block somewhere safe, flat and out of direct sunlight until you are ready to sew the whole quilt top together.

BLIND STITCH APPLIQUÉ METHOD

This hand sewing method (aka blind ladder stitch) is a super neat way to appliqué your EPP rings to the background fabric squares.

Thread a hand sewing needle and tie a knot at one end of the thread. Insert the needle from the back of the background fabric square, very close to the edge of the ring.

Insert the tip of the needle sideways into the edge of the ring; the needle should run along inside the creased edge and not pierce through to the top side of the ring. Pierce the needle back through the underside of the EPP ring, catching a small section (no more than ¼in/0.6cm) of the ring's turned-in seam allowance for a secure stitch. Then pass the needle through the background fabric, moving the needle tip along on the underside no more than ¼in (0.6cm), before bringing it through to the front of the background fabric, ready to insert the tip of the needle sideways into the edge of the ring again. Repeat all the way around. If the seam allowances of the EPP shapes overhang the front of the ring at any point, tuck them back under the ring before stitching over them to secure.

Once complete, pass the needle back through to the reverse side of the background fabric and knot to secure.

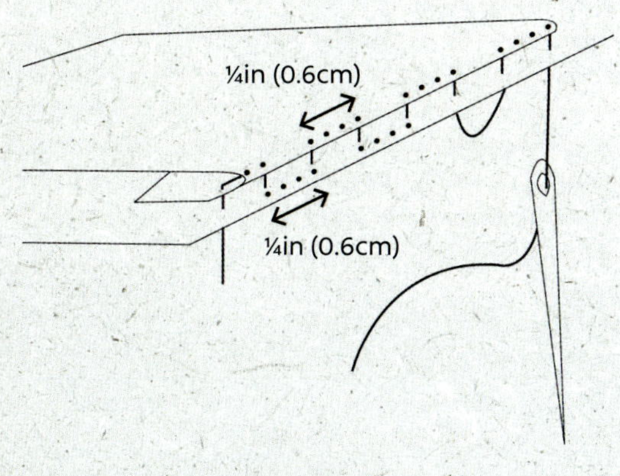

FOR HALF EPP RING

1. Take one of the background fabric right-angle triangles and press it flat. Find the centre of the triangle by folding it in half and creasing the fold line well. Unfold.

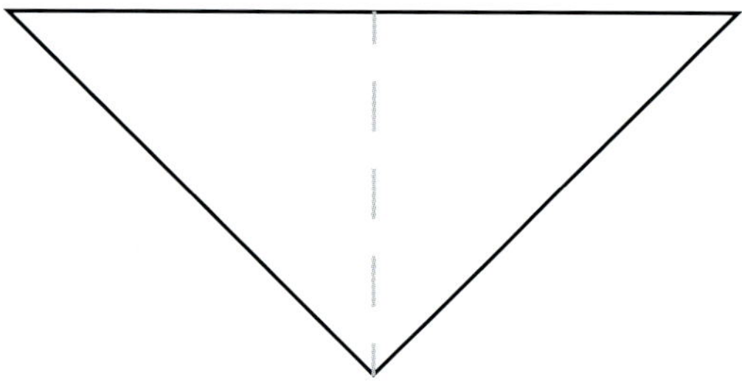

2. Use an erasable fabric marker to mark a point 4⅞in (12.4cm) up from the corner along this creased line.

4⅞in
(12.4cm)

3. Take a completed half EPP ring and arrange it flat on top of the background fabric triangle, right side up. Align the fold line with the pointed tips of the central diamond shape. Align the marked 4⅞in (12.4cm) point with the base of the central diamond shape. Note that the edges of the shapes at either side of the half ring will overhang the fabric by a small amount. Pin the half ring in place.

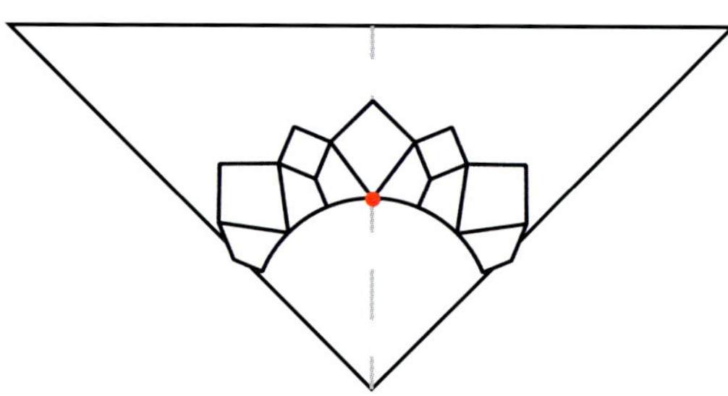

4. Use blind stitch to appliqué the top and bottom edges of the half EPP ring in place as indicated by the red lines in the enlarged diagram shown here (see Blind Stitch Appliqué Method), tucking any overhanging seam allowances under the ring as you sew. Store the completed block somewhere safe, flat and out of direct sunlight until you are ready to sew the whole quilt top together.

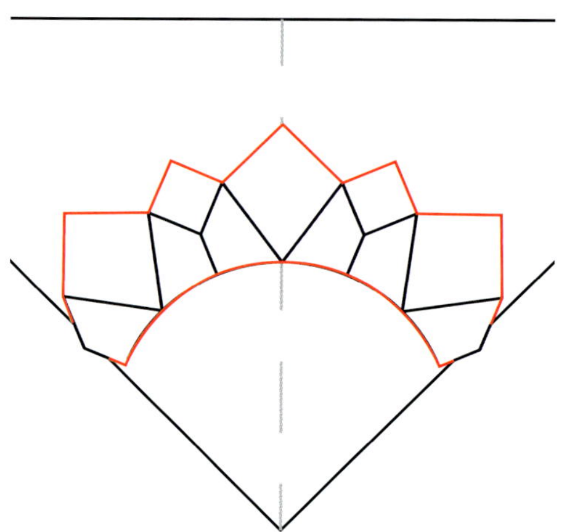

CIRCLE TEMPLATE

Actual size

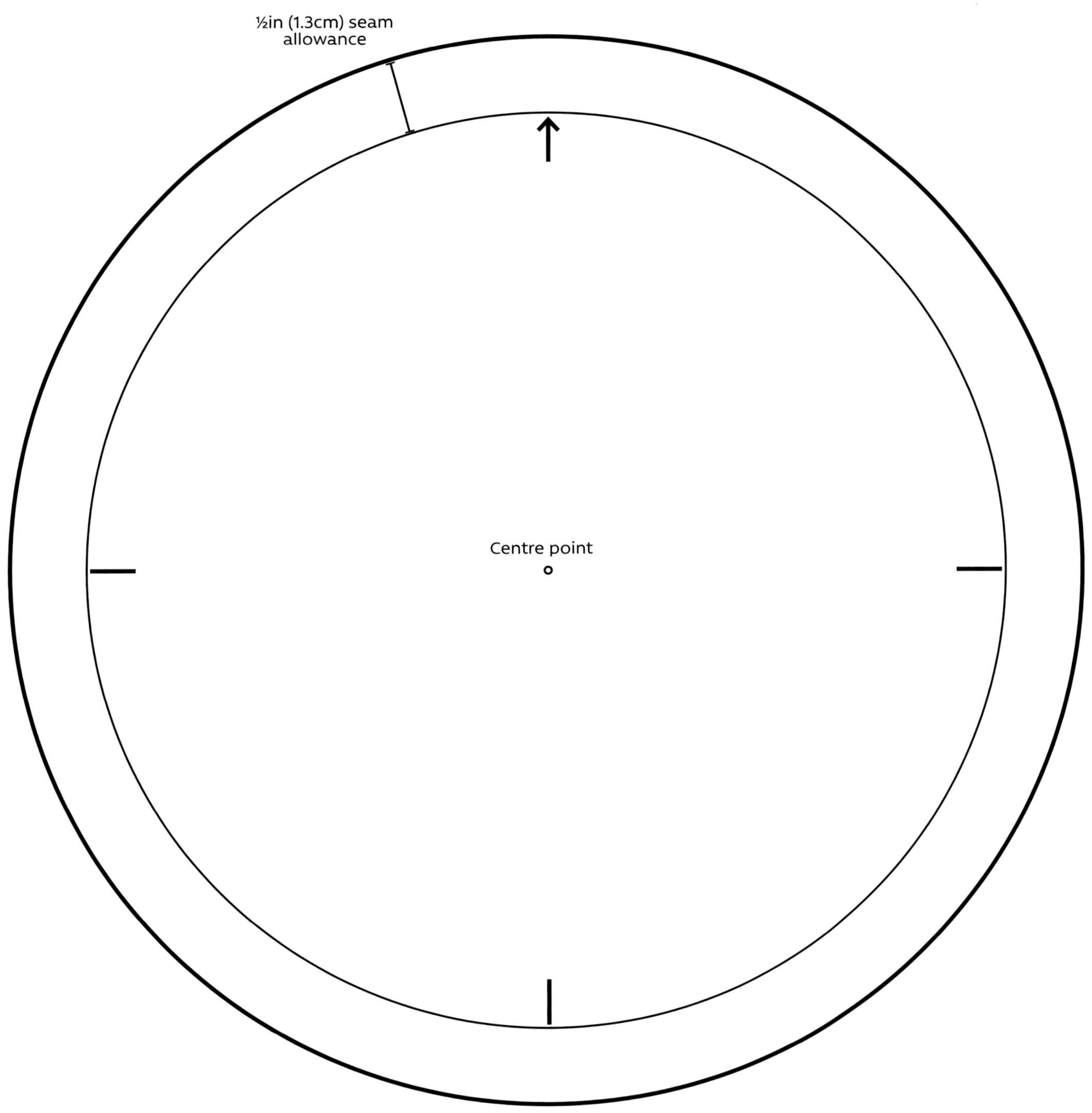

Block Layout Guides

This chapter is a visual reference for how to assemble the full ring EPP embroidery blocks and the half ring EPP border blocks to create a finished quilt as seen in the Quilt Layout Guide. For the pastel fabrics, follow the fabric chart name.

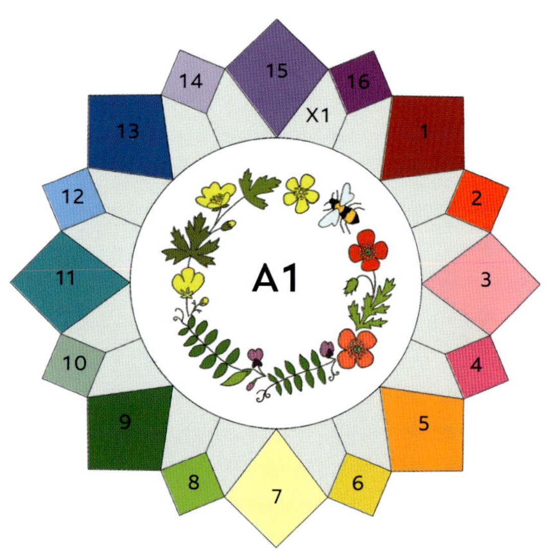

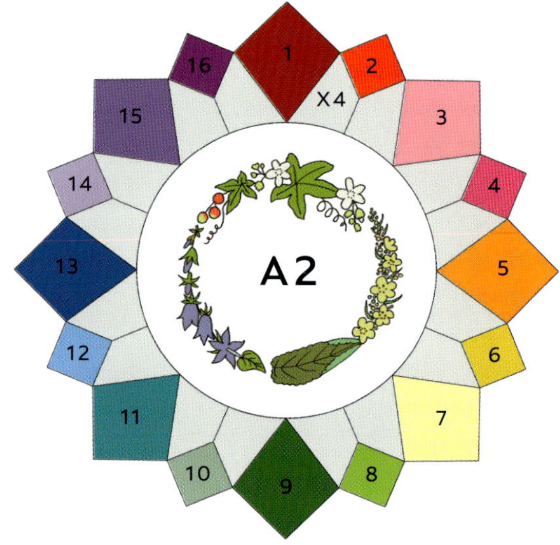

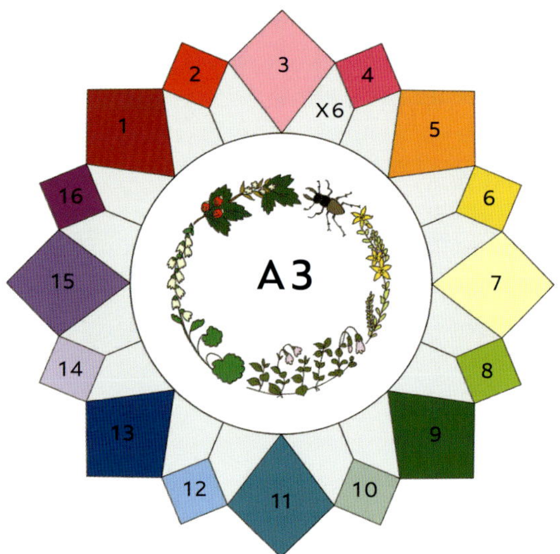

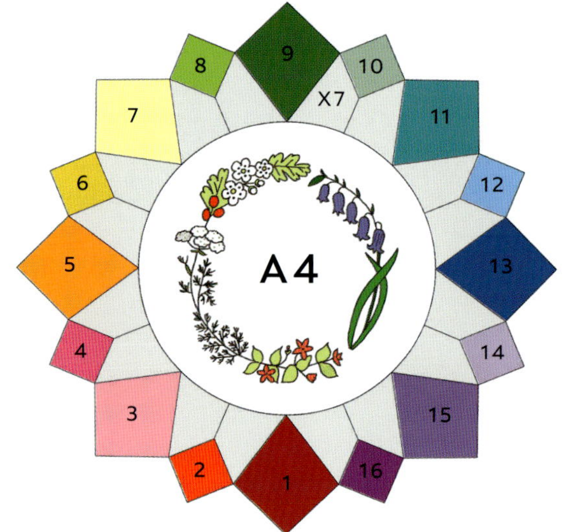

QUILT LAYOUT GUIDE

A5
X9
1
2
3
4
5
6
7
8
9
10
11
12
13
14
15
16
A6
X12
A7
X3
A8
X10
A9
X8
B1
X3

B2
X12
B3
X13
B4
X1
B5
X11
B6
X5
B7
X8

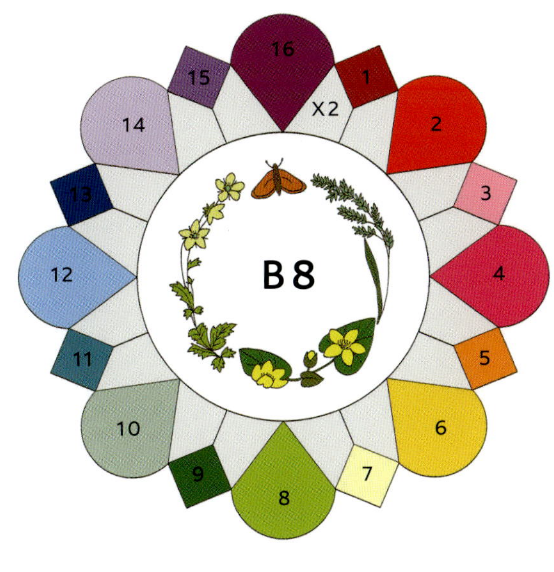
B8
X2
16
1
2
3
4
5
6
7
8
9
10
11
12
13
14
15

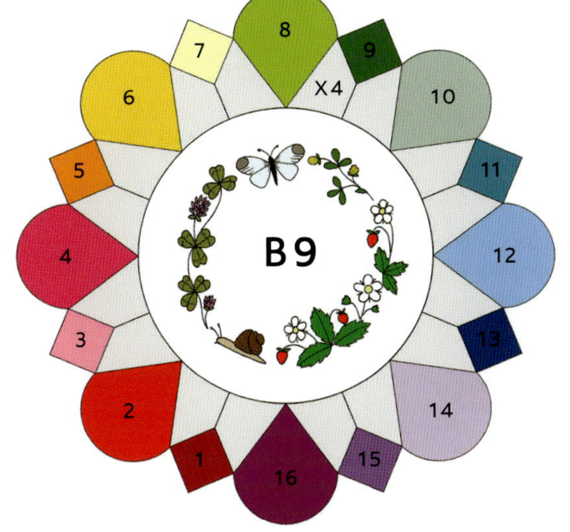
B9
X4
8
9
10
11
12
13
14
15
16
1
2
3
4
5
6
7

B10
X11
8
9
10
11
12
13
14
15
16
1
2
3
4
5
6
7

B11
X7
2
3
4
5
6
7
8
9
10
11
12
13
14
15
16
1

B12
X9
6
7
8
9
10
11
12
13
14
15
16
1
2
3
4
5

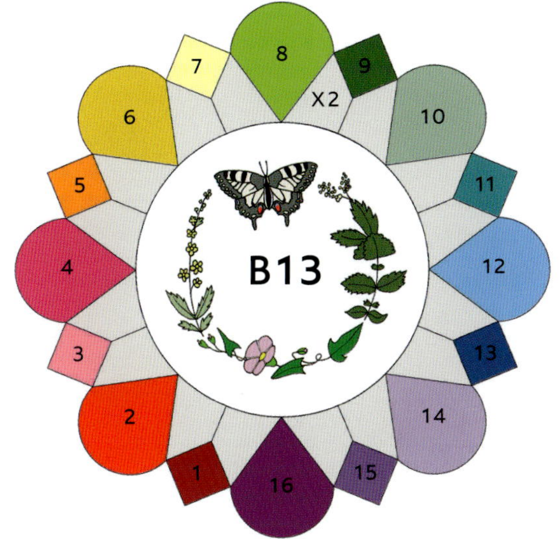
B13
X2
8
9
10
11
12
13
14
15
16
1
2
3
4
5
6
7

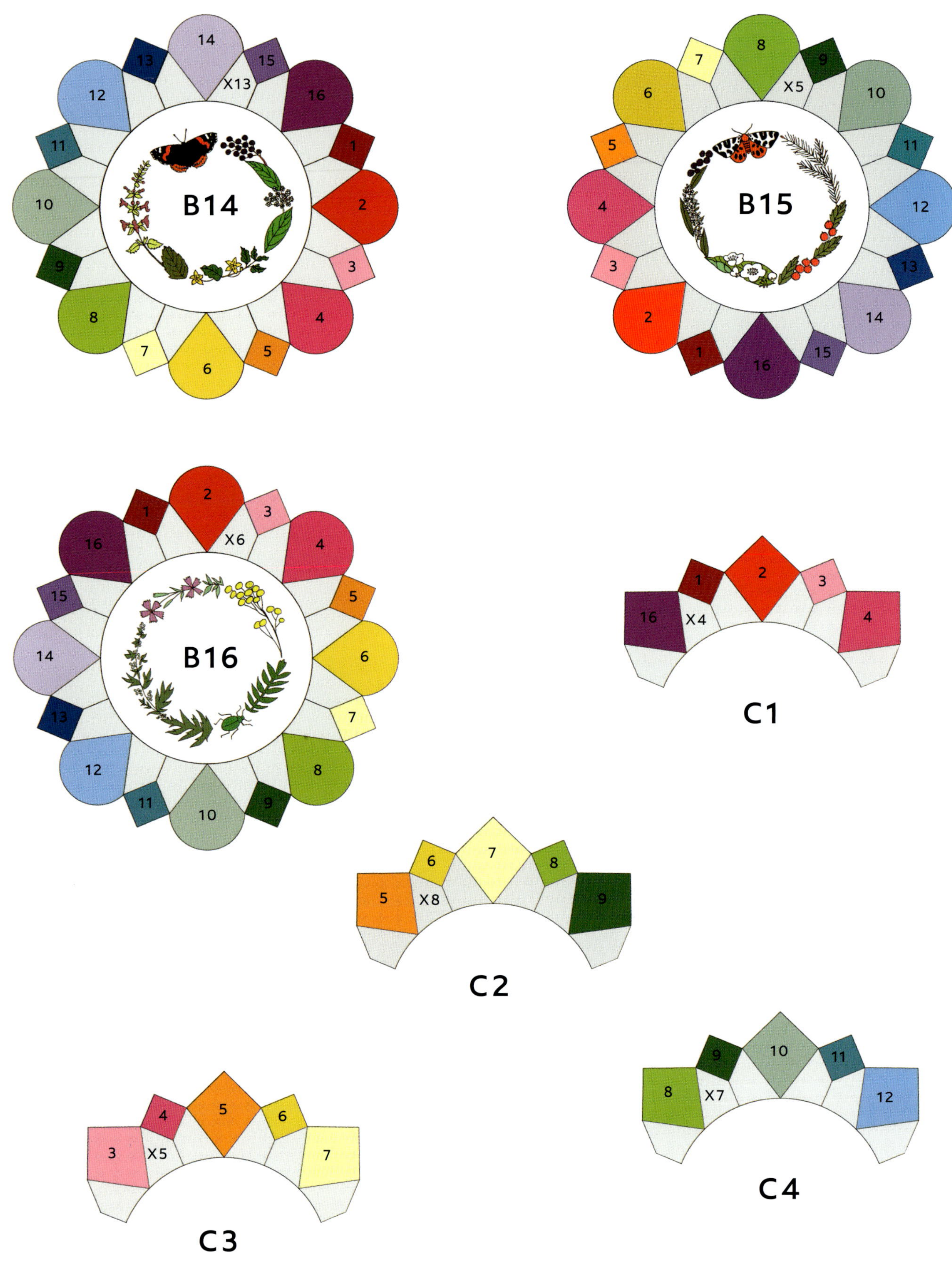
B14
X13
B15
X5
B16
X6
C1
X4
C2
X8
C3
X5
C4
X7

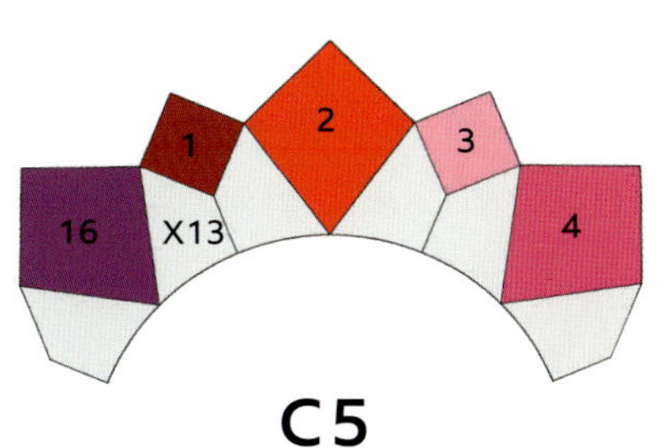

C5

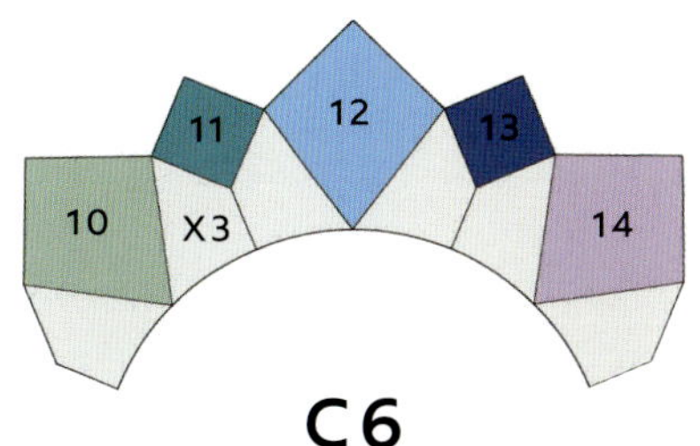

C6

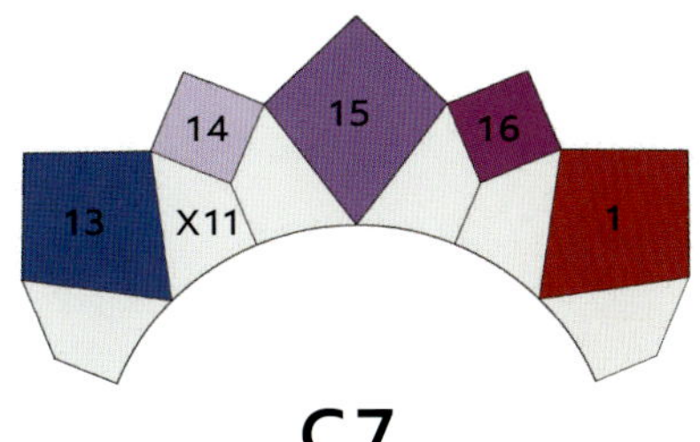

C7

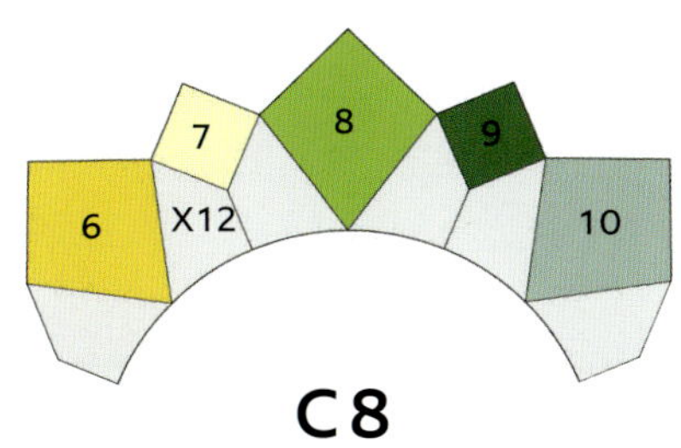

C8

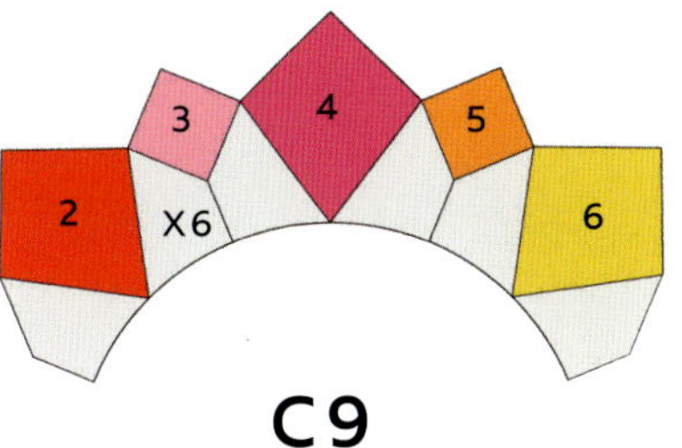

C9

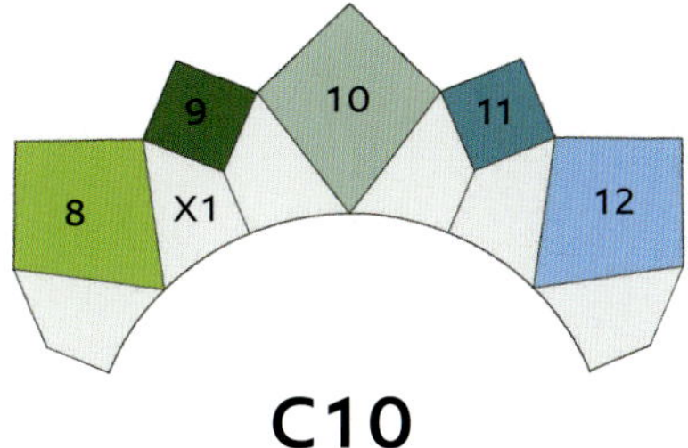

C10

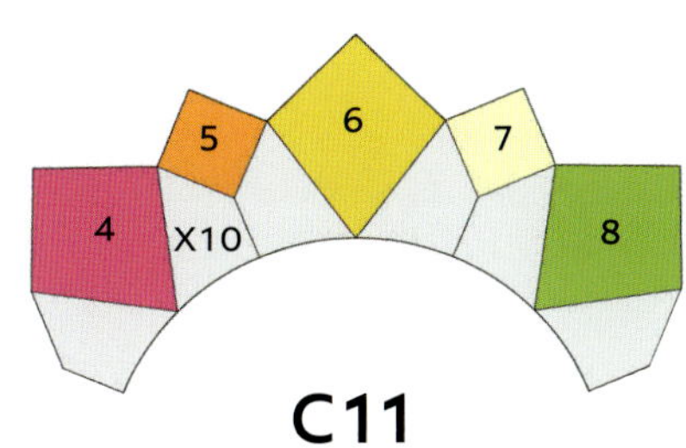

C11

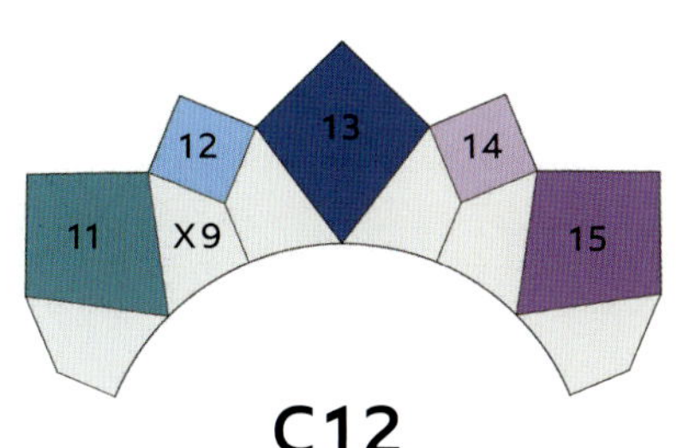

C12

Making the Quilt

Once all the blocks have been assembled, it's time to join them all together to make your final quilt. So get your sewing machine ready!

STAGE 1: MAKE THE QUILT TOP

1. Referring to the Quilt Layout Guide (see the Block Layout Guides chapter) and the finished quilt photograph shown opposite, lay out your finished blocks, paying attention to the correct orientation of each block. Sew the blocks together in diagonal rows.

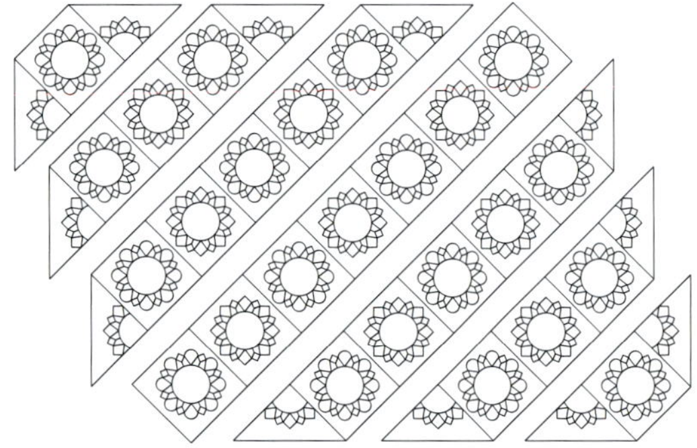

2. Sew on the remaining four small background fabric triangles to the ends of the indicated rows.

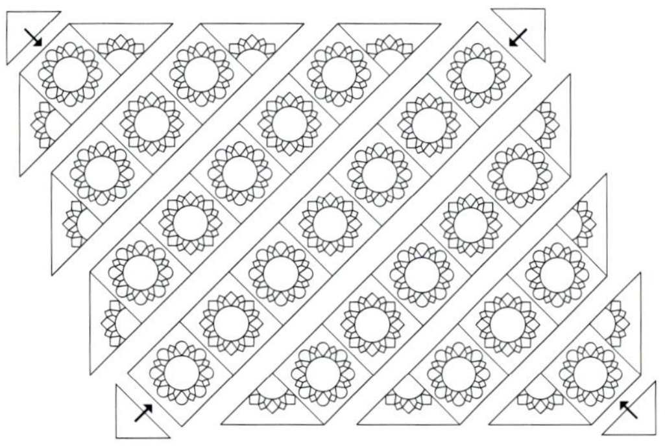

QUILT NOTES

- All seams are ¼in (0.6cm) unless stated otherwise.
- Always secure stitches at the beginning and end of your stitching.
- Always align fabric edges neatly and pin to secure before sewing.

3. These small background triangles form the corners of the quilt, and these rows now look like this.

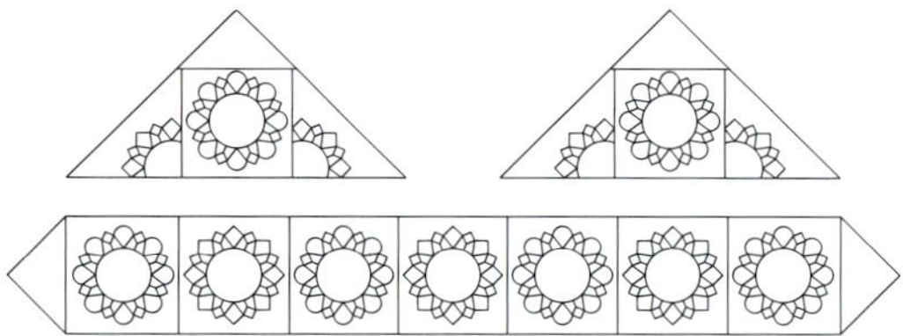

4. Now sew the rows together to complete the quilt top.

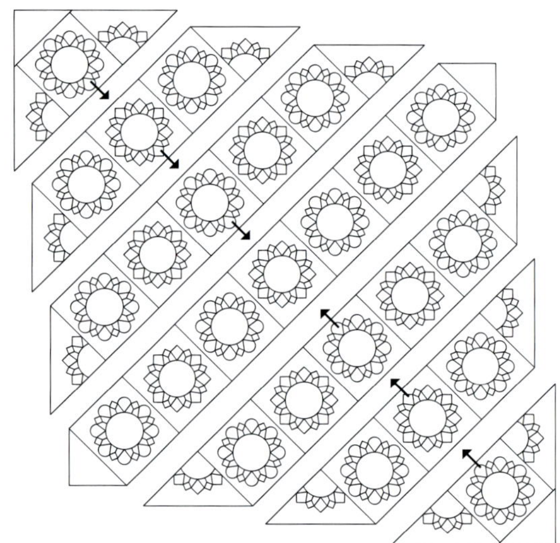

STAGE 2: MAKE A QUILT SANDWICH AND QUILT

1. First, make your quilt sandwich by layering up the backing fabric, wadding (batting) and finished quilt top. Lay the pressed backing fabric right side down on a large flat surface then lay the wadding on top. Align the edges, taking care that the backing fabric does not wrinkle or crease as the wadding is laid down. Lay the completed quilt top centrally on top of the wadding, right side facing up. You will have about a 5in (12.7cm) excess of wadding and backing fabric around the outside edges as a safety allowance for any edge that hasn't turned out completely straight; this ensures there will be no area on the front of the quilt that won't be backed by the wadding and backing fabric.

2. Tack (baste) the three layers of the quilt sandwich together with rows of stitches 8–10in (20–25cm) apart. There is no need to be neat as these stitches will be removed later.

3. Following the advice in How to Quilt and Where to Quilt, work the quilting stitches that will hold the three layers of your quilt sandwich together.

4. Once all of the quilting is complete, trim the wadding and backing fabric to be level with the quilt top. The quilt should be square with straight edges.

TIP:

Make your tacking (basting) stitches using a brightly coloured thread to ensure the stitches are easier to find and remove later. Alternatively, use quilting safety pins or wash-out fabric adhesive to hold the quilt sandwich together while you stitch.

HOW TO QUILT

Use one of the following methods, remembering that however you choose to quilt, it is important to never quilt on top of your embroidery stitches:

Straight line quilting using a sewing machine: Lines of straight stitching on the block seams as outlined in Where to Quilt are simplest. You can use the standard sewing foot on your machine, although if you invest in a walking foot, this will help guide all three layers through the machine at the same pace, therefore avoiding puckering.

Machine free-motion quilting: This is particularly good for organic, curved lines. Use a free-motion quilting foot if you have one, although a standard foot works too if you are careful. With right side of quilt facing up, draw on your design using an erasable fabric marker or buy templates to follow, then get stitching using a slightly longer stitch length than normal (3.5–4). For detailed designs, fitting a large embroidery hoop around the area will help to keep it taut but be careful of your embroidered areas.

Hand quilting: Use a 'sharp' or 'between' quilting needle (gold-tipped is best) and Aurifil 50wt thread. Place the area you wish to quilt inside a large embroidery hoop to keep it from creasing and moving the layers out of place, carefully avoiding the embroidery; don't pull the fabric completely taut within the hoop as you will need to be able to manipulate the fabric as you stitch. Thread your needle and tie a knot at the end of the thread. Bring the needle from the back of the quilt to the front, then pass it back through to the back of the quilt. Keep your stitches even and consistent – we recommend five stitches per inch. You can sew several stitches at a time before pulling the needle through. When you run out of thread, take your needle to the back of the quilt and knot against the backing fabric, or make three small stitches on top of each other to secure. Rethread the needle and start again.

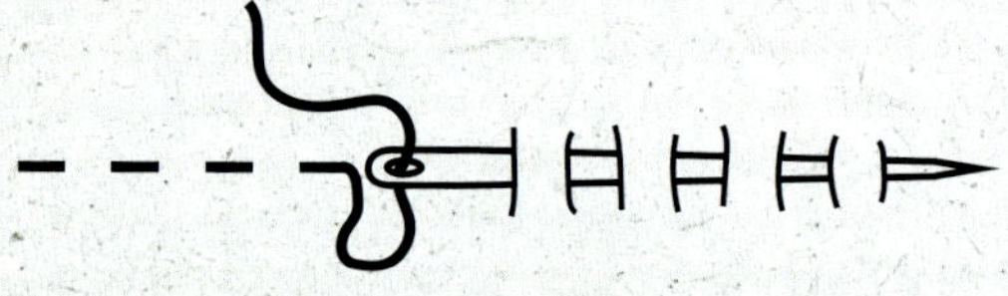

When hand quilting, keep stitch length consistent and work several stitches at a time.

WHERE TO QUILT

If you are unsure about where to quilt, we recommend using straight line quilting by machine or hand and stitching as described here, in a variety of thread colours. An optional hand quilting detail can then be worked between the blocks:

For full blocks not on the edges of the quilt: Using various coloured threads, stitch ⅛in (0.3cm) inside from the edge of the block's outer straight seam (A).

For full blocks around the edge of the quilt: Stitch only along the two edges that face in towards the quilt centre (B).

For full blocks in the corners of the quilt: Stitch only along the edge that faces in towards the quilt centre (C).

For optional hand quilting detail: Use an erasable fabric marker to trace on the simple flower design (see Quilt Flower Template) at the 'X' point where four block seams meet (marked in blue on the template) and hand quilt in a variety of thread colours.

TIP:

If you do not wish to complete the quilting yourself, you could have it quilted by a professional long-arm quilting company, as we have done on our quilt. You may find one local to you. They will be able to offer a library of different quilting patterns to choose from and can even quilt bespoke designs.

QUILT FLOWER TEMPLATE

Actual size

STAGE 3: BIND THE QUILT

Choose one of the following two methods to bind your quilt with your binding strips:

MACHINE FINISHING

1. Along one edge of each binding strip, fold over ¼in (0.6cm) onto the wrong side. Press.

2. Align the unfolded side of one binding strip against one edge of the quilt back, right sides of fabric together. Pin in place and sew the binding to the reverse of the quilt, ¼in (0.6cm) from the edge.

3. Press the binding out to the side and then fold it around the raw edge of the quilt to the front. Turn the quilt over and, ensuring that the binding covers up the stitches from step 2, topstitch the folded edge of the binding to the front of the quilt. On the back, your stitches should lie next to the binding. Trim the ends of the binding level with the top and bottom edges.

4. Repeat steps 2 and 3 on the opposite side of the quilt with another binding strip.

5. Take another binding strip and repeat step 2 along the top edge on the back of the quilt, this time leaving at least ⅜in (1cm) of the binding strip overhanging the quilt at both ends.

6. Press the binding up to the top and then fold both overhanging ends of the binding around the edge of the quilt to the front. Fold the rest of the binding strip down over the top edge, towards the front of the quilt and covering the raw edge. Topstitch, ensuring the stitches made in step 5 are covered.

7. Repeat steps 5 and 6 at the bottom edge of the quilt with the remaining binding strip.

Sew binding strip along unfolded edge to one side of the back, right sides together

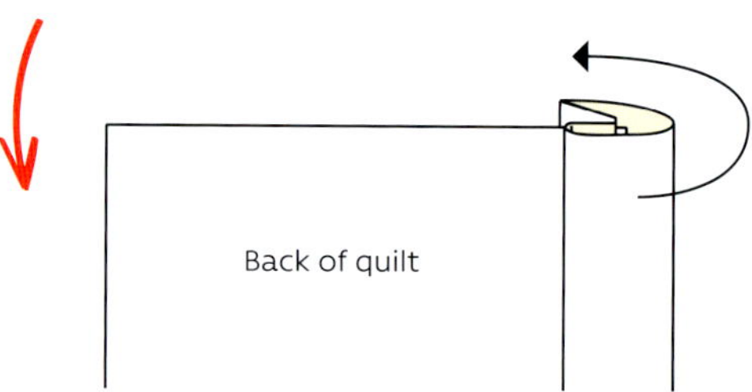

Press out and bring around to the front

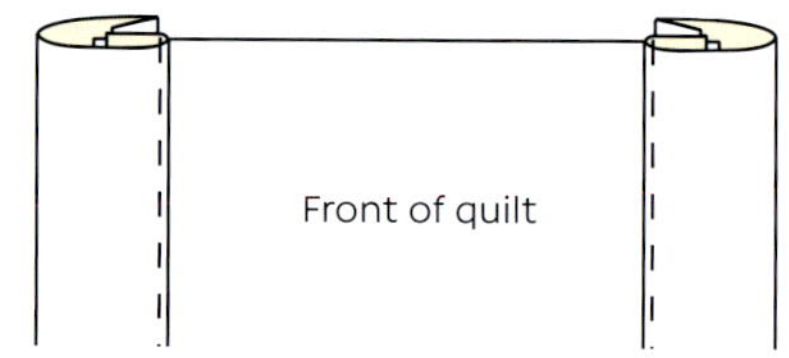

Topstitch the strip down on the front; add binding strip to opposite side in the same way

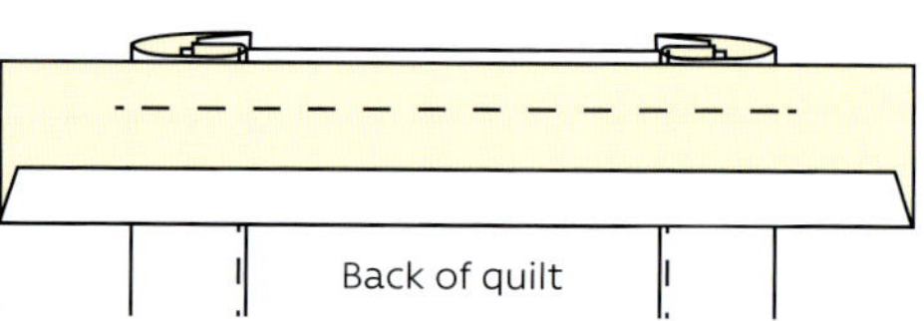

Sew binding strip to the top edge of the back

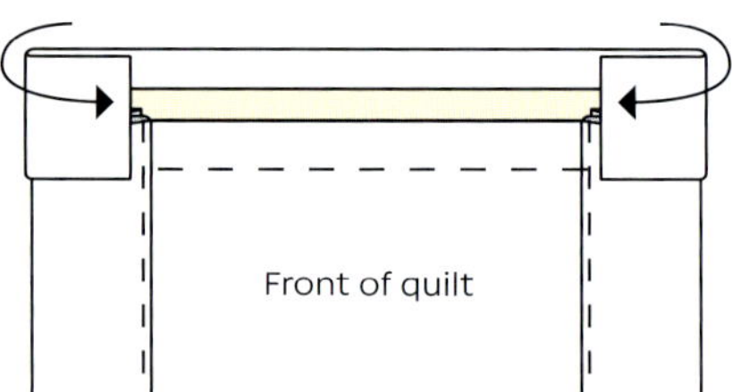

Press up and bring the edges around to the front

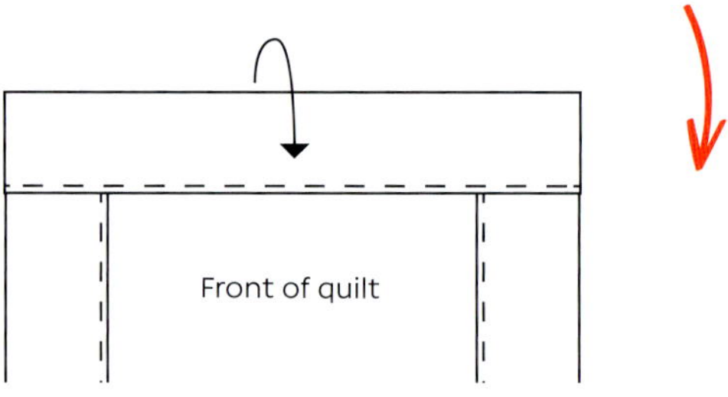

Fold the strip down over the top edge and sew

HAND FINISHING

Follow the Machine Finishing instructions as written but with the following alterations:

In step 2: Align the unfolded side of one binding strip against one edge of the quilt *front*, right sides of fabric together.

In step 3: Press the binding out to the side and then fold it around the raw edge of the quilt to the *back*. Then, use blind stitch by hand with a needle and thread to hand sew the folded edge of the binding to the quilt on the *back*. This results in a very neat and clean finish, with no stitching visible on the binding at the front or back.

In step 5: Sew the binding strip to the *front* of the quilt.

In step 6: Fold both overhanging ends of the binding around the edge of the quilt to the *back*. Then, fold the rest of the binding strip down over the top edge, towards the *back* of the quilt. Use blind stitch by hand to sew the binding strip down, leaving no visible stitching.

In step 2, sew the binding strip to one side of the *front*

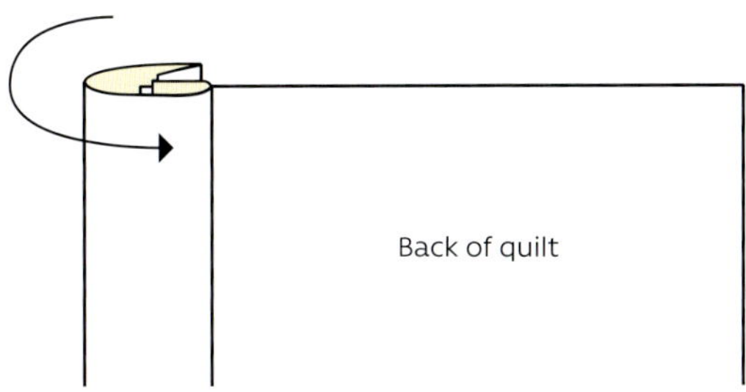

In step 3, press the binding out and bring around to the *back*

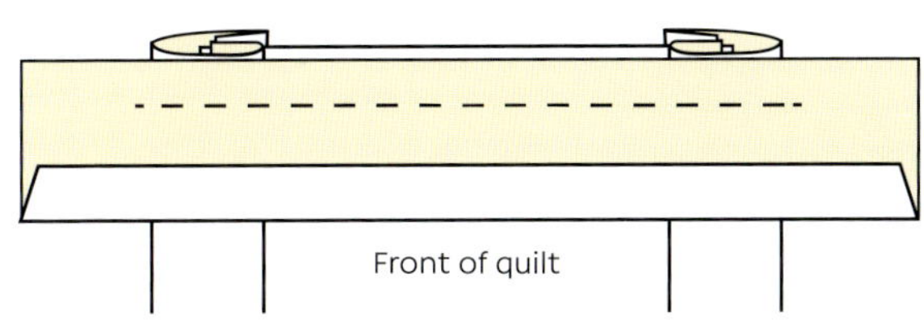

In step 5, sew the binding strip to the top edge of the quilt *front*

TIP:

If you need to complete a quilt fast, machine finishing the binding is a good choice but stitching will be visible on the front of the quilt. For a neat, clean look, hand finishing the binding is the way to go. It will take longer to complete but the results are well worth the effort as it leaves no visible stitching.

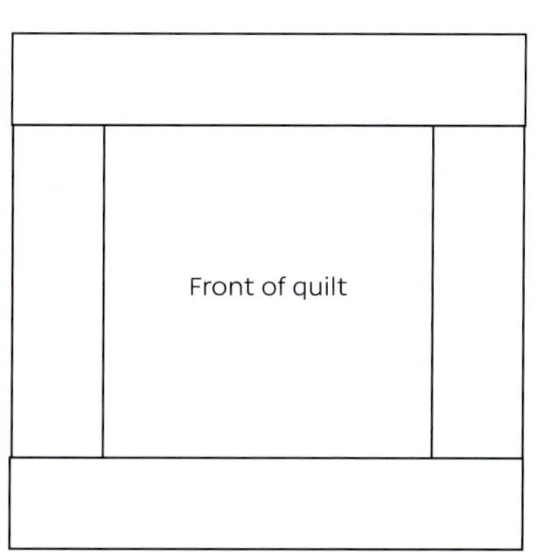

In step 6, blind stitch by hand to finish the binding on the *back* so there is no visible stitching on the front (or back!) of the quilt

The Embroideries

The embroideries featured in Alice's Country Diary Quilt were inspired by my countryside walks and I very much enjoyed time spent back in the studio researching my nature finds. To get the best results, please refer to the information below when stitching these designs.

STITCH NOTES

Unless stated otherwise, please complete the embroidery designs following these guidelines:

- Use two strands of thread.
- Use satin stitch to fill shapes.
- Use back stitch for leaf veins.
- Use couching for stem lines: for the anchoring thread always use only one strand even when the number of strands used for the laid thread varies from two (see Embroidery Techniques: Couching).
- Always stitch the background fill stitch (e.g. satin stitch, split back stitch) before any top details (e.g. back stitch, straight stitch, French knots).
- Where a particular direction has been indicated for the stitches this applies to all like shapes.
- Where a particular stitch and/or thread colour has been indicated this applies to all like areas.
- Where a variegated thread is required, as for the tortoiseshell butterfly on Block B11, follow the annotating instructions to mix the thread strands required.

TIPS FOR EMBROIDERY

- A good light source is essential for accurate, neat work. Sew by a window during the day or use a lamp with a daylight bulb. Make sure you can see the traced or transferred pattern easily and that your eyes are not straining.
- Sit on a comfortable chair and take care of your posture. When embroidering, the upper back tends to become hunched and shoulders and arms tense, so sit up straight with your shoulders back and legs bent at 90 degrees. Stand up for a short time if you can once an hour to re-set your posture.
- Our eyes can become strained when doing intense close work for long periods, so do look up from your embroidery at least once every half hour, to focus on objects further away for at least 30 seconds. Setting an alarm will help you to remember to do this.
- Regularly check your stitching. If you notice an error in the stitches you have just made, unthread the needle and gently pull out the stitches using the needle. Rethread the needle and stitch again. Errors found later are more difficult to correct, so we'd recommend embracing the imperfect and leaving them in. It is handmade and unique after all!
- When finishing an embroidery session, always loosen the tension significantly on the embroidery hoop. This will prevent the fabric from stretching out of shape. When starting another session, simply tighten the hoop again.

A NOTE ON FORAGING

When foraging, it's essential that you correctly identify the plants you are picking, particularly if you intend to eat them! Always seek positive identification from multiple sources. Best of all, I would recommend that you take a locally guided foraging walk from an expert.

Block A1

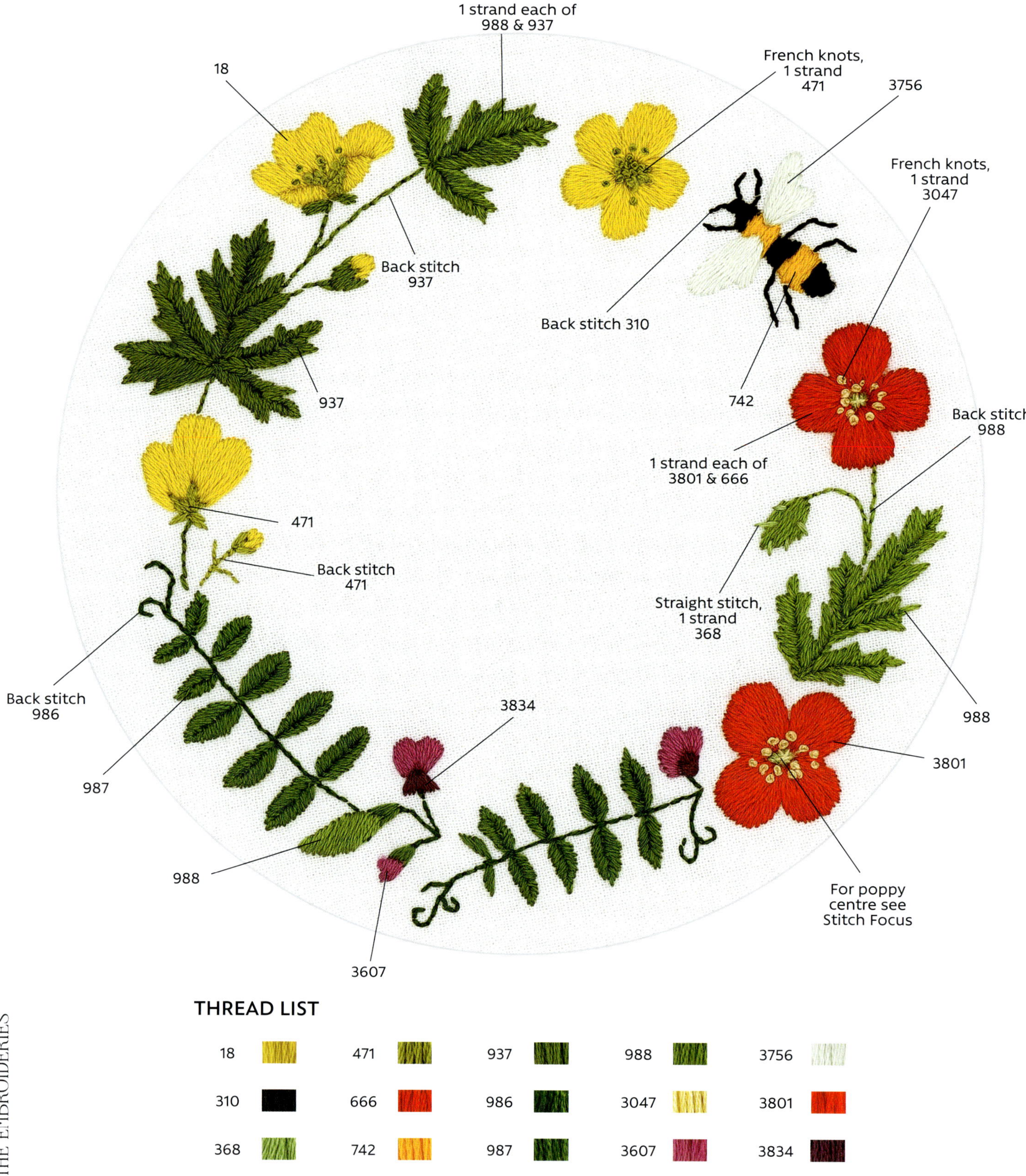

THREAD LIST

18	471	937	988	3756
310	666	986	3047	3801
368	742	987	3607	3834

STITCH FOCUS

The distinctive centre of the poppy flower is stitched first in satin stitch with 368, then straight stitches are worked on top with 3047.

In the wild, honey bees live in wooded areas in large hives made of wax honeycombs. A single beehive may contain as many as 50,000 individuals. In winter, the hive goes into survival mode: the drones are expelled, the workers huddle together to keep warm, and the larvae are fed on stores of pollen and honey. In spring, a new generation of bees emerges. It takes twelve bees their entire lifetime to make a teaspoon of honey!

FLORA AND FAUNA KEY

1 Meadow buttercup

2 Honey bee

3 Long smooth-headed poppy

4 Common vetch

Block A2

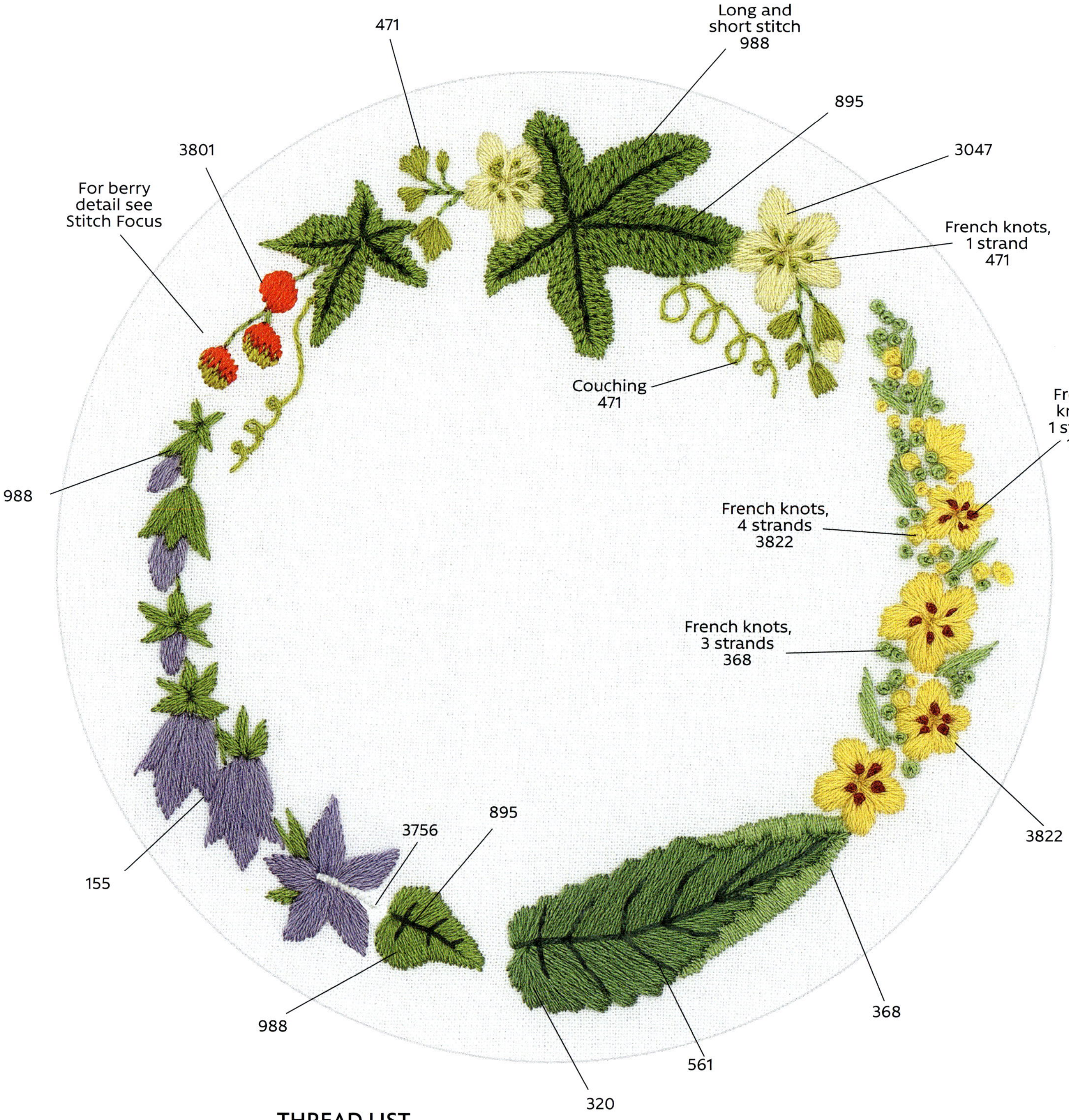

471

Long and short stitch 988

895

3801

3047

For berry detail see Stitch Focus

French knots, 1 strand 471

Couching 471

988

French knots, 1 strand 150

French knots, 4 strands 3822

French knots, 3 strands 368

155

3756

895

3822

988

368

561

320

THREAD LIST

150		368		895		3756	
155		471		988		3801	
320		561		3047		3822	

STITCH FOCUS

White bryony produces garlands of red berries just in time for Christmas! To create the authentic detailing of the fruit, use long and short stitch to mix 3801 and 471 in the needle to shade where the two colours join.

Creeping bellflower is native to Europe and western Siberia, where it grows in semi-shaded areas, such as open woods and the edges of denser forests, and meadowland. This pretty flower is considered an invasive weed in the USA as it is very difficult to remove. Historically grown for food, the roots, leaves and shoots are all edible, if a little bland.

FLORA AND FAUNA KEY

1 White bryony

2 Great mullein

3 Creeping bellflower

Block A3

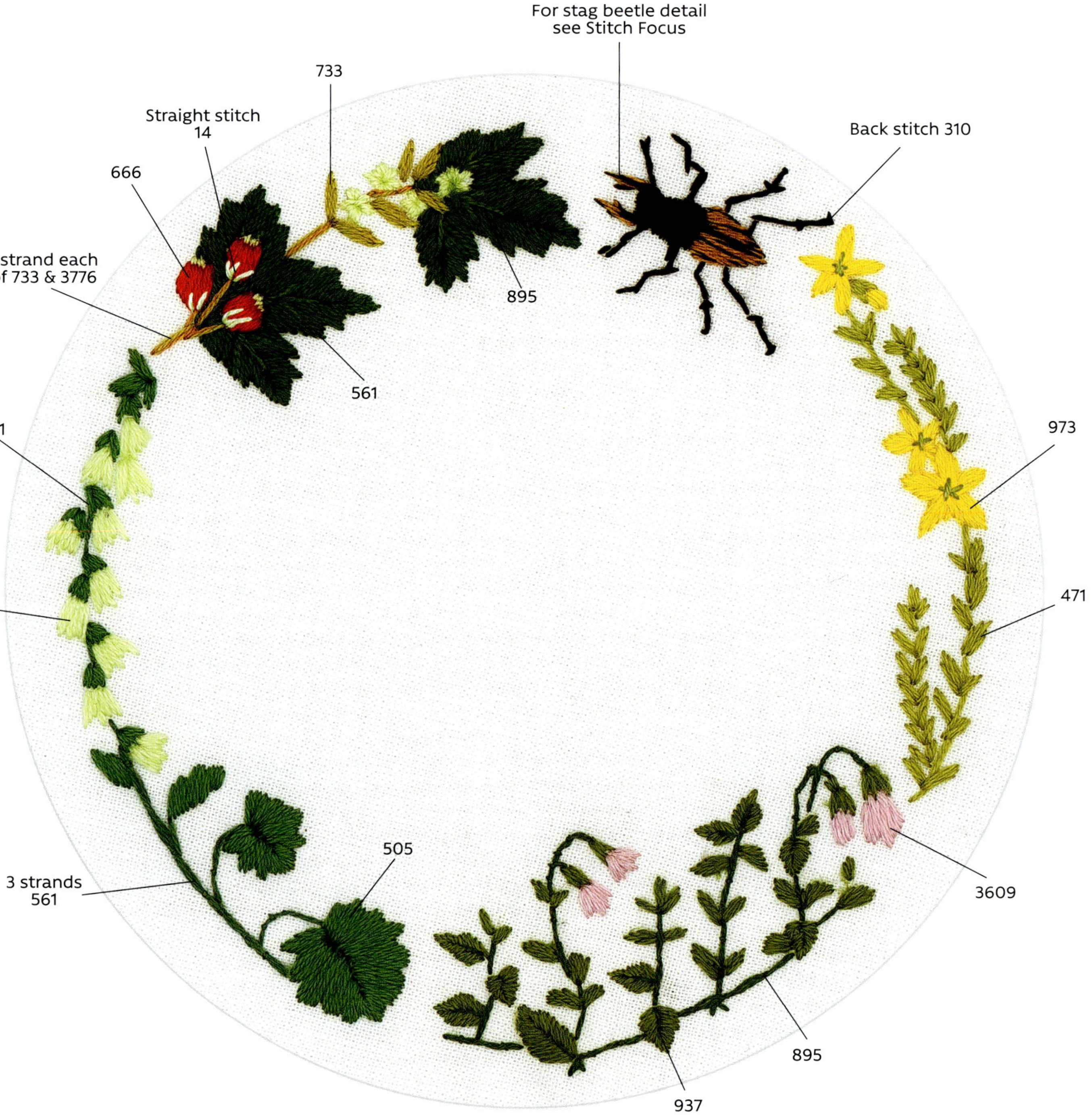

For stag beetle detail see Stitch Focus

733

Straight stitch 14

Back stitch 310

666

1 strand each of 733 & 3776

895

561

561

973

14

471

505

3 strands 561

3609

895

937

THREAD LIST

14		505		733		973	
310		561		895		3609	
471		666		937		3776	

STITCH FOCUS

The stag beetle is one of the most magnificent beetles in the UK – the male's large jaws look just like the antlers of a stag! To stitch these and the beetle's wing caps, use one strand each of 310 and 3776 in your needle. To stitch the rest of the body, use satin stitch and 2 strands of 310.

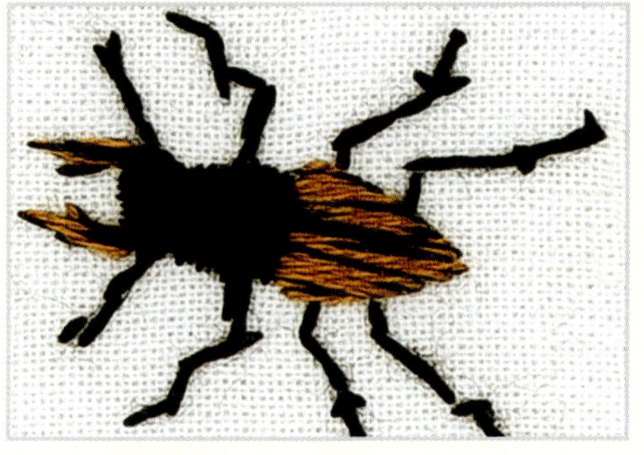

Goldmoss stonecrop is a tiny, tuberous-rooted, carpet-forming, evergreen succulent perennial, commonly found on well-drained ground, such as sand dunes, shingle, grasslands, walls and pavements. The fleshy leaves have an unexpected biting-hot taste!

Block A4

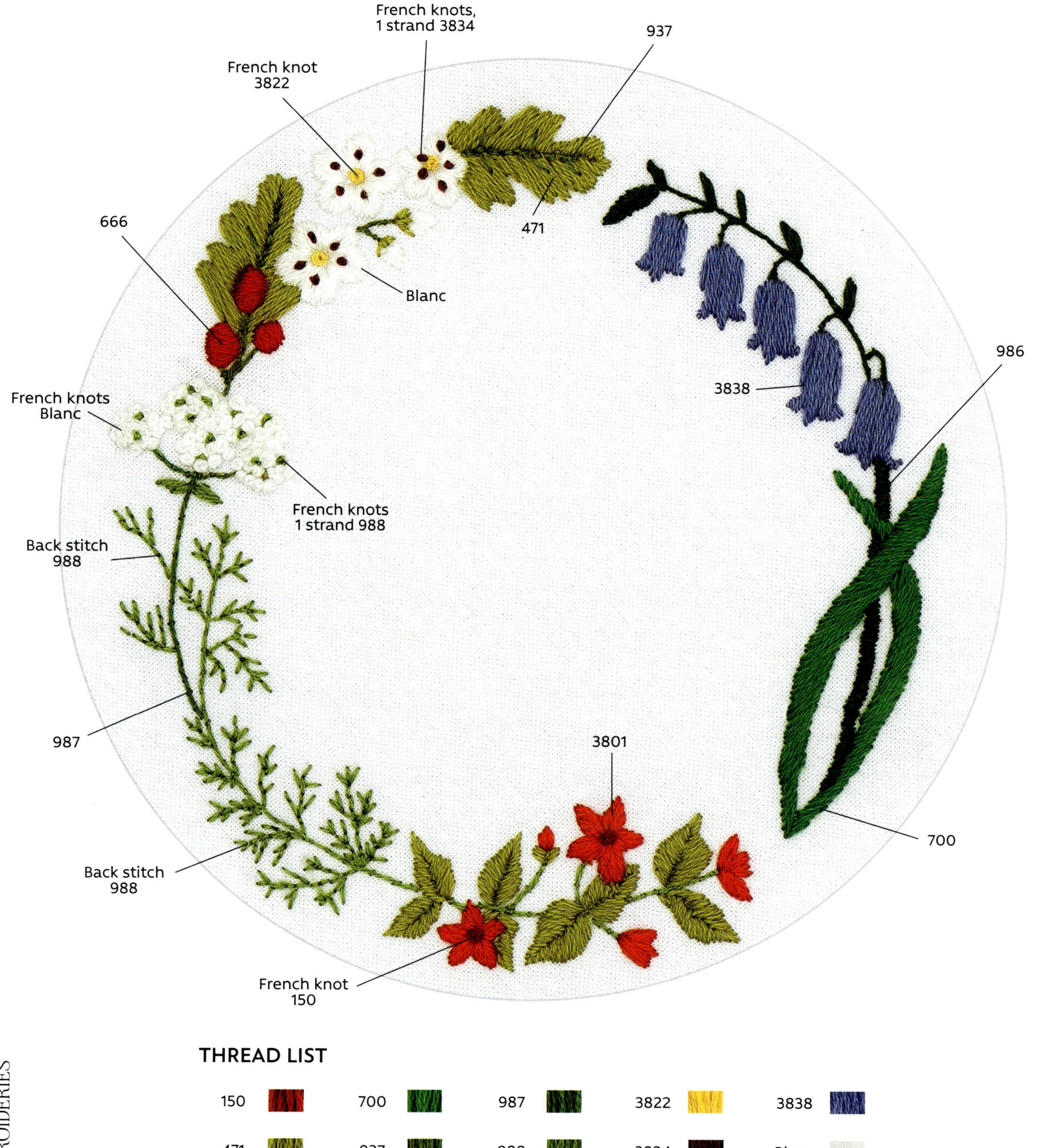

THREAD LIST

150		700		987		3822		3838	
471		937		988		3834		Blanc	
666		986		3801					

STITCH FOCUS

The tiny scarlet pimpernel, a childhood favourite of mine, provides a study in the importance of directional stitching when working satin stitch. Observe the photo carefully to replicate the buds, petals and leaves of this delightful wildflower.

The sight of a bluebell carpet in a woodland in late spring is such a joy to behold! On a warm day the scent is delightful and may waft upwards to greet you. The UK is home to more than half the world's population of bluebells, making it our unofficial national flower.

Block A5

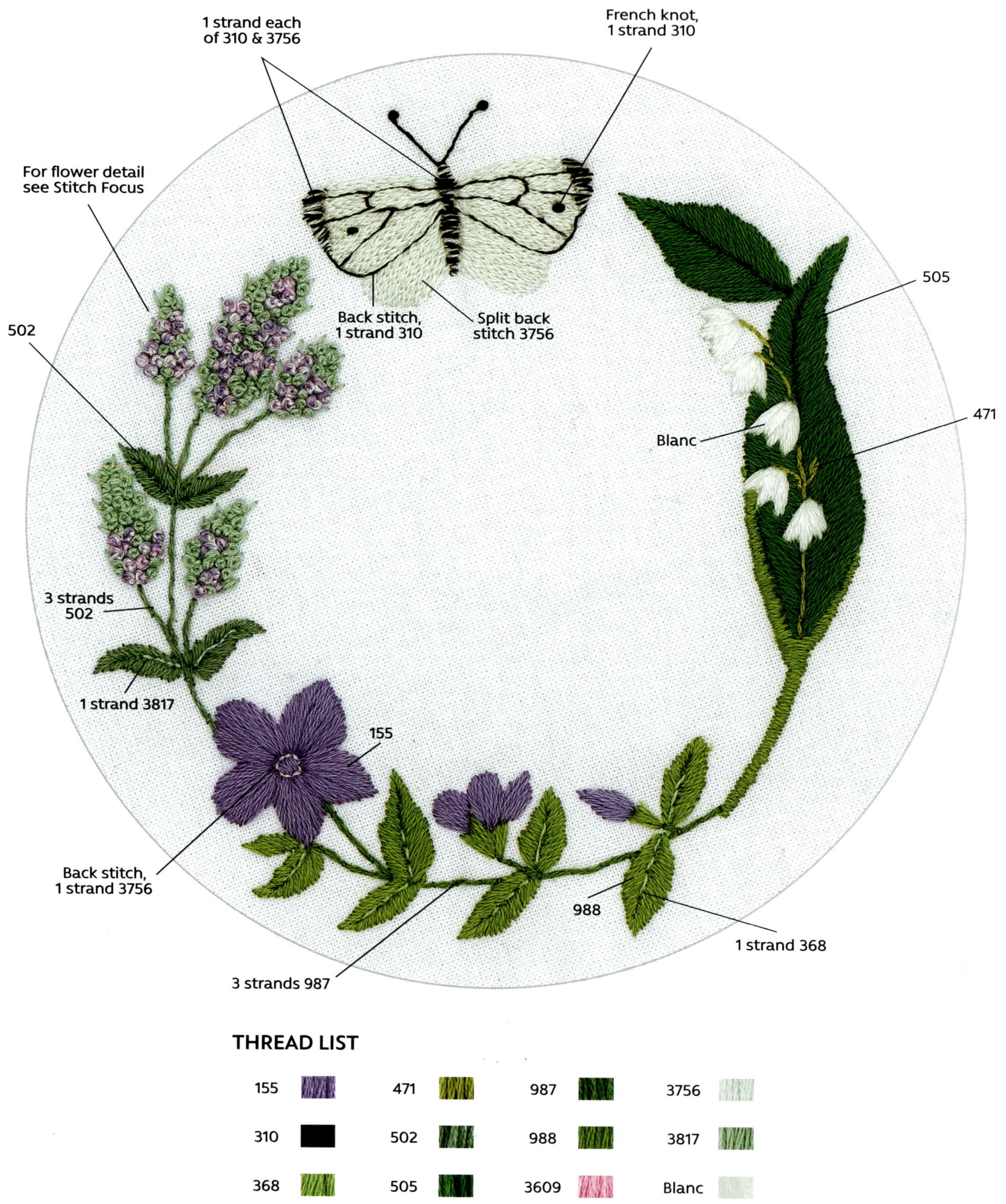

THREAD LIST

155	471	987	3756
310	502	988	3817
368	505	3609	Blanc

STITCH FOCUS

Stitch the dense spikes of the horsemint flowers in the following order: (1) French knots in clusters of four, using one strand each of 155, 3756 and 3609 in the needle; (2) fill remaining background shape with single 3817 French knots, with two strands; (3) straight stitches on top, with one strand of 3817.

Stitch the background detail of the butterfly wings first, using split back stitch and 3756 to fill in direction indicated in the diagram.

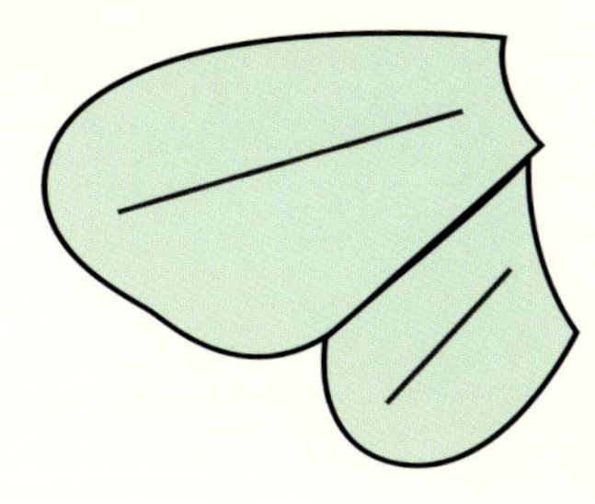

The green-veined white butterfly, often mistaken for the small white butterfly, is white on its top side and green underneath. It can be found in a wide variety of habitats including gardens, although it prefers damp areas with lush vegetation. One of the most widespread species found in the British Isles, it can be found almost everywhere, except certain parts of northern Scotland.

Block A6

French knots
742

471

18

150

Back stitch,
1 strand 310

733

895

1 strand each
of Blanc & 310

3755

French knots
3822

Back stitch
33

Straight stitch,
1 strand Blanc

Straight stitch
310

368

Back stitch
368

320

895

French knots
988

18

988

Back stitch
733

THREAD LIST

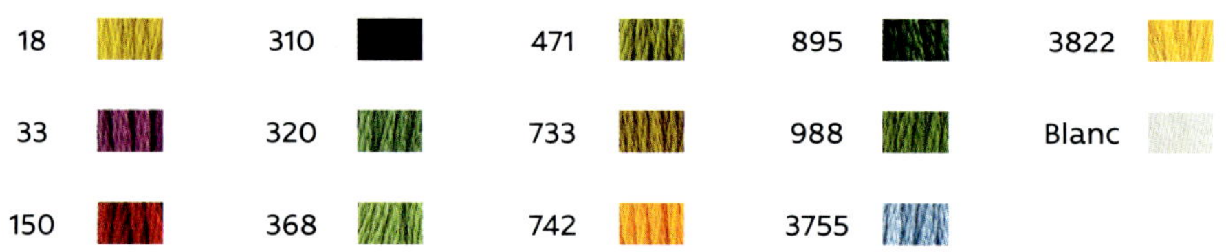

18	310	471	895	3822
33	320	733	988	Blanc
150	368	742	3755	

STITCH FOCUS

Once the satin stitch base of the greater knapweed flower has been stitched, work its purple, thistle-like florets with back stitch, then finish with the single straight black stitches that help to define the centre of the flower head.

The forget-me-not is traditionally a symbol of enduring love and fidelity. Adopted by the English monarch King Henry IV as his royal emblem during his exile in 1398, this pretty little blue flower was, for him, a sign of royalty and endurance.

Block A7

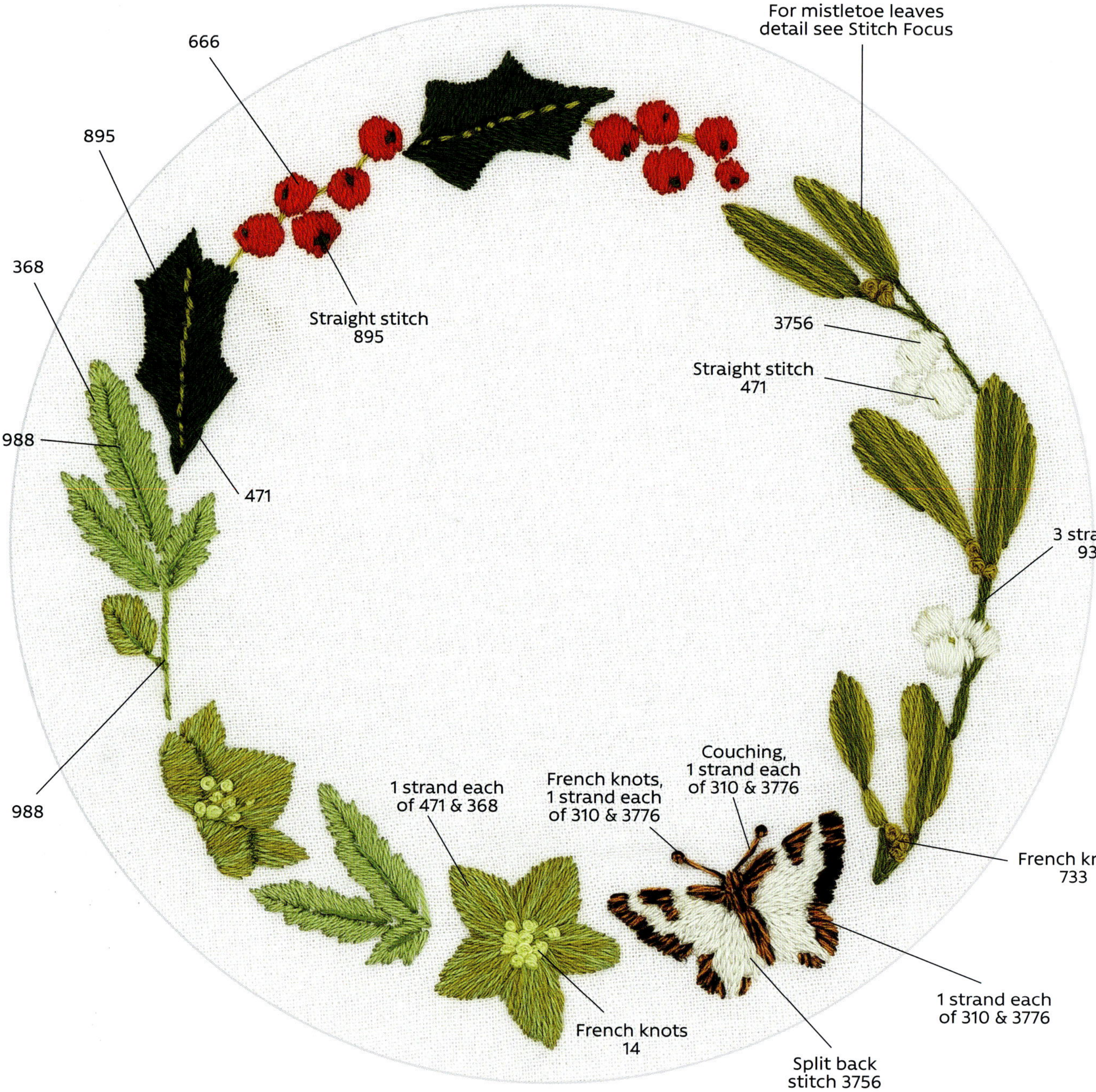

666

895

368

988

471

Straight stitch
895

988

For mistletoe leaves
detail see Stitch Focus

3756

Straight stitch
471

3 strands
937

Couching,
1 strand each
of 310 & 3776

French knots,
1 strand each
of 310 & 3776

1 strand each
of 471 & 368

French knots
733

1 strand each
of 310 & 3776

French knots
14

Split back
stitch 3756

THREAD LIST

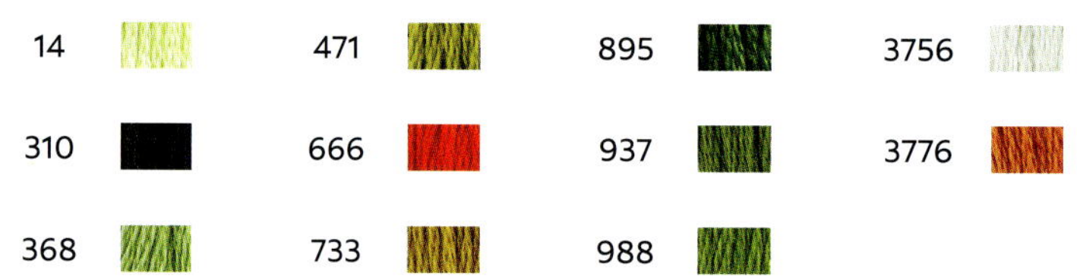

STITCH FOCUS

It's a Christmas tradition to kiss under the mistletoe – with 900 species of the plant, there's plenty of opportunity for that! For the mistletoe leaves, first fill with satin stitch using 471, then work the couching on top with 937.

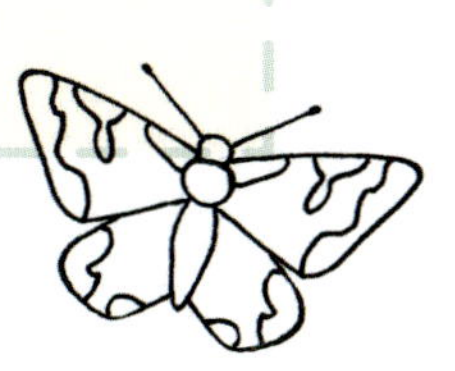

Holly trees can live for up to 300 years! Superstition, magic and myth surround this plant. The Druids, Celts and Romans brought evergreens such as holly into their homes during winter. They believed the ability of these plants to keep their leaves was magical and assured the return of spring.

Block A8

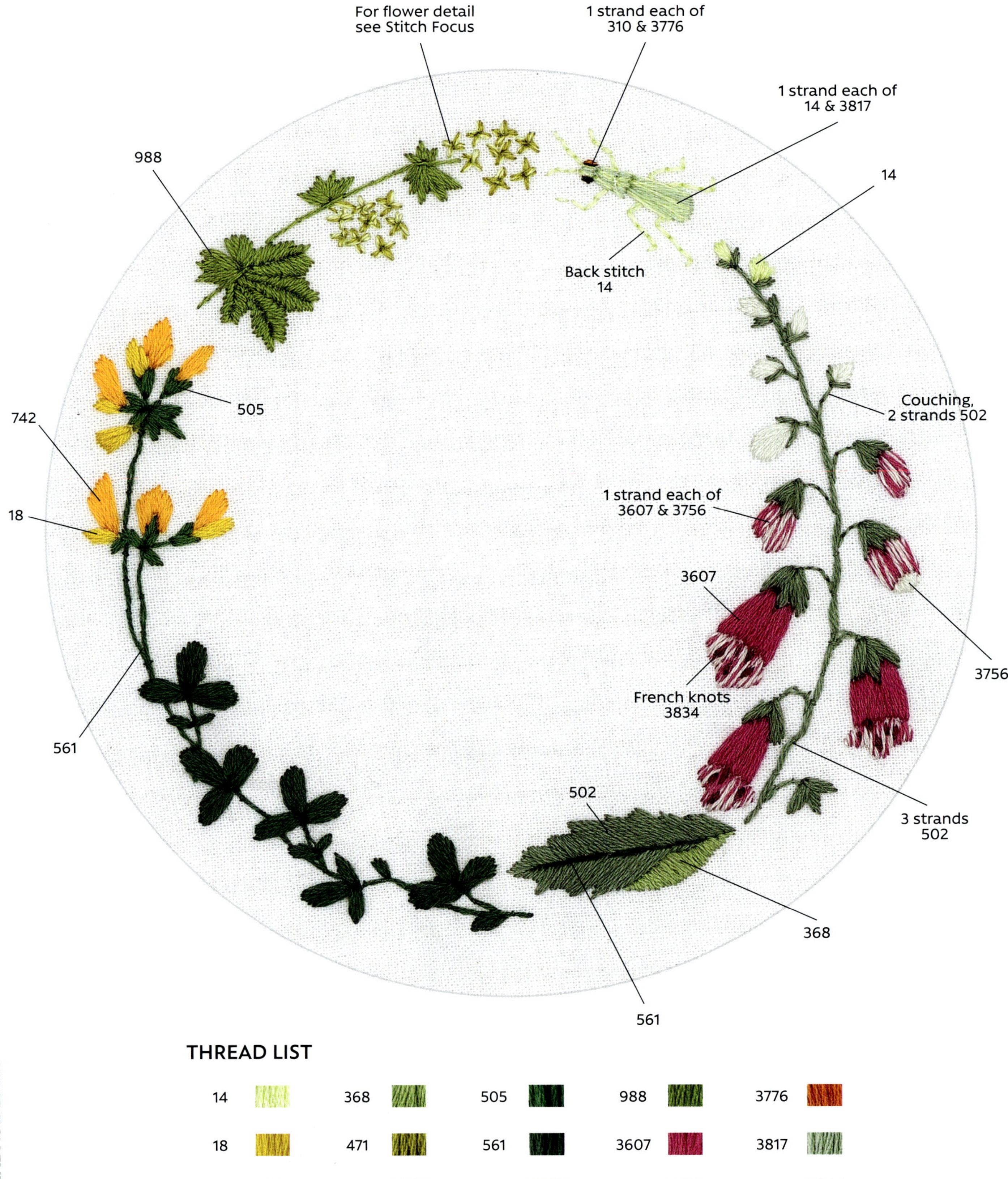

THREAD LIST

14	368	505	988	3776
18	471	561	3607	3817
310	502	742	3756	3834

STITCH FOCUS

The delicate colouring of the lady's mantle flowers has been captured by mixing threads in the needle, using one strand each of 14 and 471. Colour mixing has also been used to achieve the almost transparent sheen of the insect's body (14 and 3817) as well as to suggest the roundness of its side-of-head eyes (310 and 3776).

Majestic foxgloves are a wonderful sight but handle with care! They contain a chemical called digoxin which is toxic, with even small amounts causing unpleasant effects, even death in some cases. Digoxin is also a very useful drug, most commonly used to treat abnormal heart rhythms, and it is still extracted from foxgloves today.

Block A9

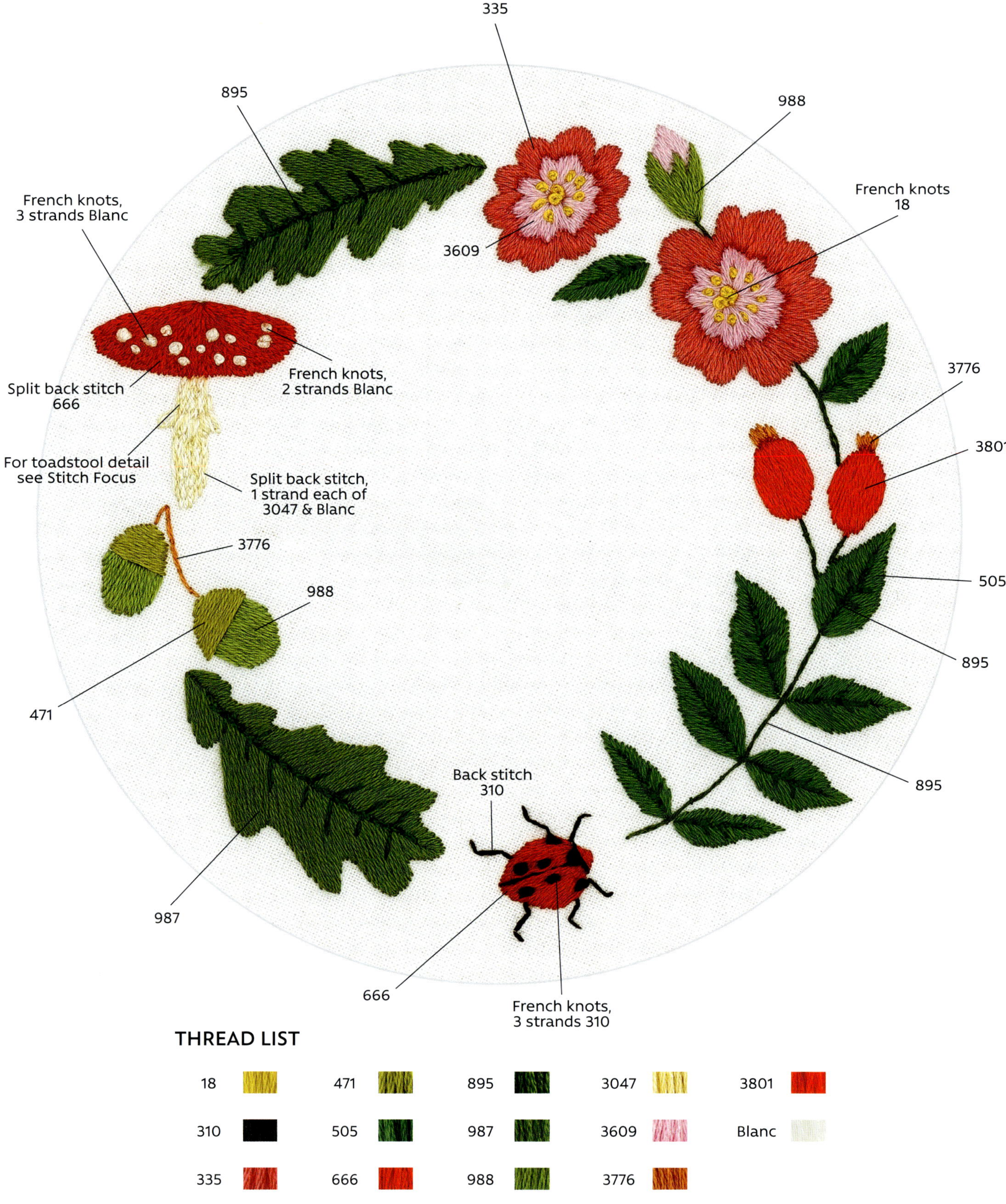

THREAD LIST

18	471	895	3047	3801
310	505	987	3609	Blanc
335	666	988	3776	

STITCH FOCUS

Work the cap of the toadstool with split back stitch using two strands of 666 in the direction indicated by the lines on the diagram. The stalk (also worked in split back stitch but note the change of direction) uses one strand each of Blanc and 3047 in the needle, and the annulus (veil remnant) is worked with the same thread mix for the single lazy daisy stitches.

The dog rose is the most abundant of the UK's native wild roses, with sweet-scented pink or white flowers that appear in June and July. Rosehips have more vitamin C than oranges and during World War II, more than 500 tons were collected every year by Boy Scouts, Girl Guides, the Women's Institute and even schoolchildren.

Block B1

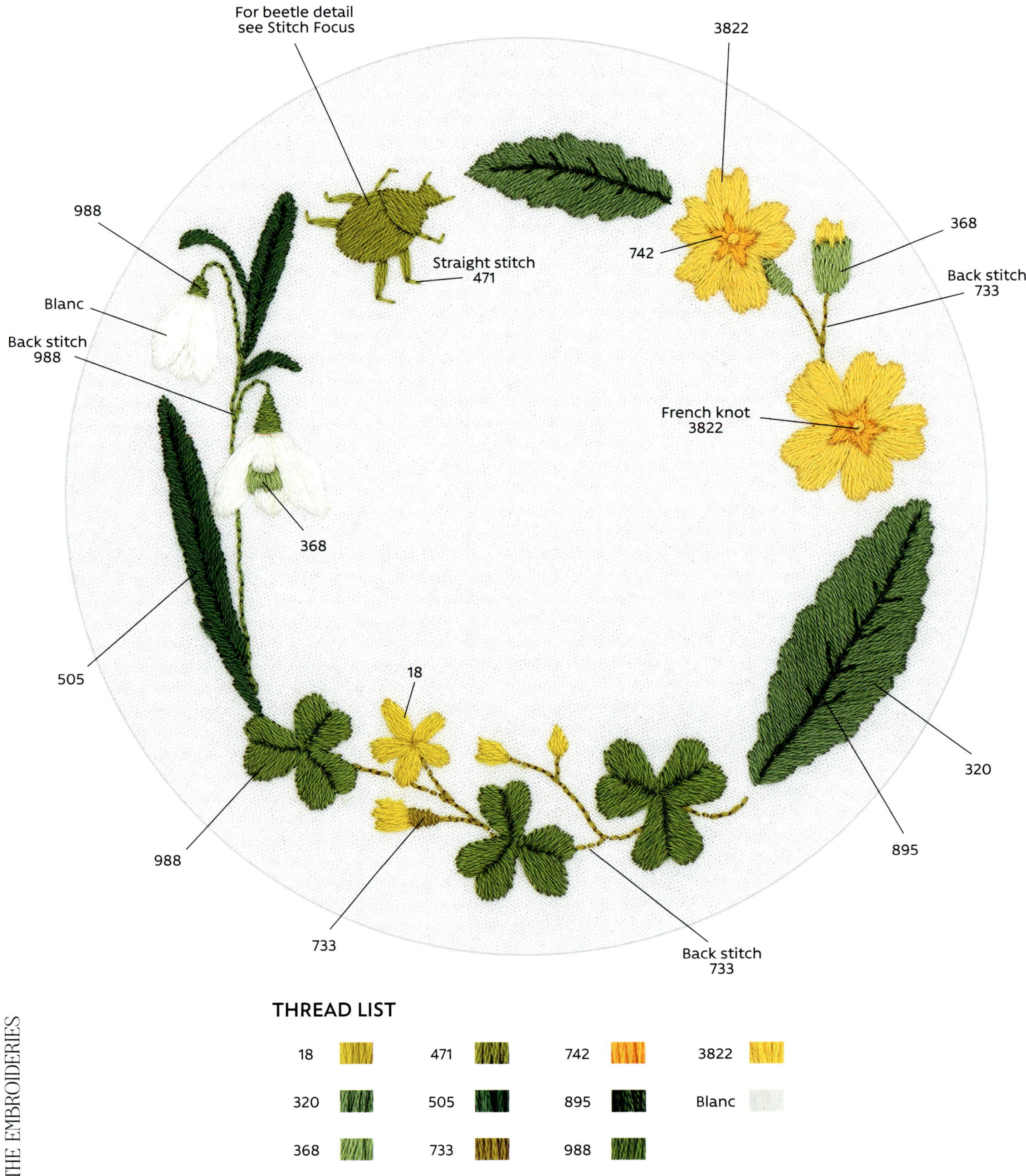

THREAD LIST

18		471		742		3822	
320		505		895		Blanc	
368		733		988			

STITCH FOCUS

Getting the direction of your satin stitch right when stitching the common sun beetle is key to achieving the metallic sheen it is well-known for, so follow the diagram carefully as shown, using 471.

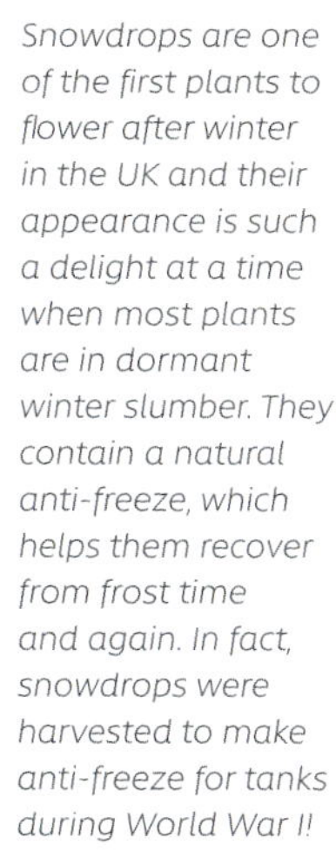

Snowdrops are one of the first plants to flower after winter in the UK and their appearance is such a delight at a time when most plants are in dormant winter slumber. They contain a natural anti-freeze, which helps them recover from frost time and again. In fact, snowdrops were harvested to make anti-freeze for tanks during World War I!

Block B2

Back stitch 3776

French knots 310

French knots 3776

French knots 742

Split back stitch 310

742

Back stitch 18

French knots 561

561

3609

3607

For colour mixing detail for butterfly body & wings see Stitch Focus

Straight stitch 702

18

973

702

Blanc

986

THREAD LIST

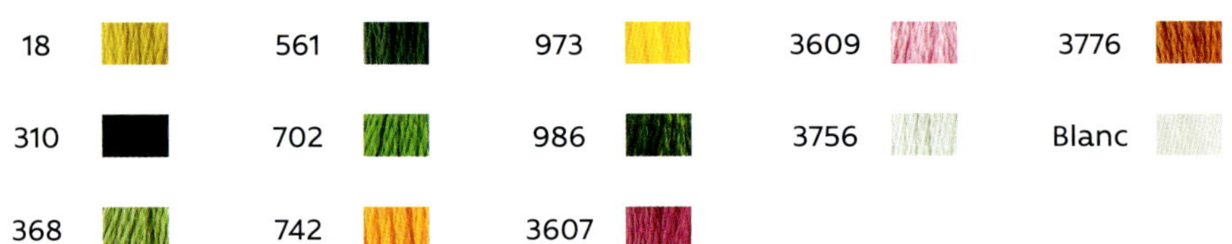

18	561	973	3609	3776
310	702	986	3756	Blanc
368	742	3607		

STITCH FOCUS

Colour mixing in the needle is used to the full to achieve the beautiful colouring of the clouded yellow butterfly. For the thorax (upper body) use one strand each of 310 and 368; for the abdomen (lower body) use one strand each of 368 and 3756; and for the inner section of the hindwing (lower wing) use one strand each of 368 and 742.

The flowers of the tuberous pea are such a glorious bright magenta pink that it is a delight to find. One has grown for decades in the verge on my Dad's farm and I was wondering why it had never spread further than its usual patch. Apparently, the pea seed pods are particularly hard to germinate. They need a mouse to nibble them, Dad says, or a knife nick in the pod in order to do so.

Block B3

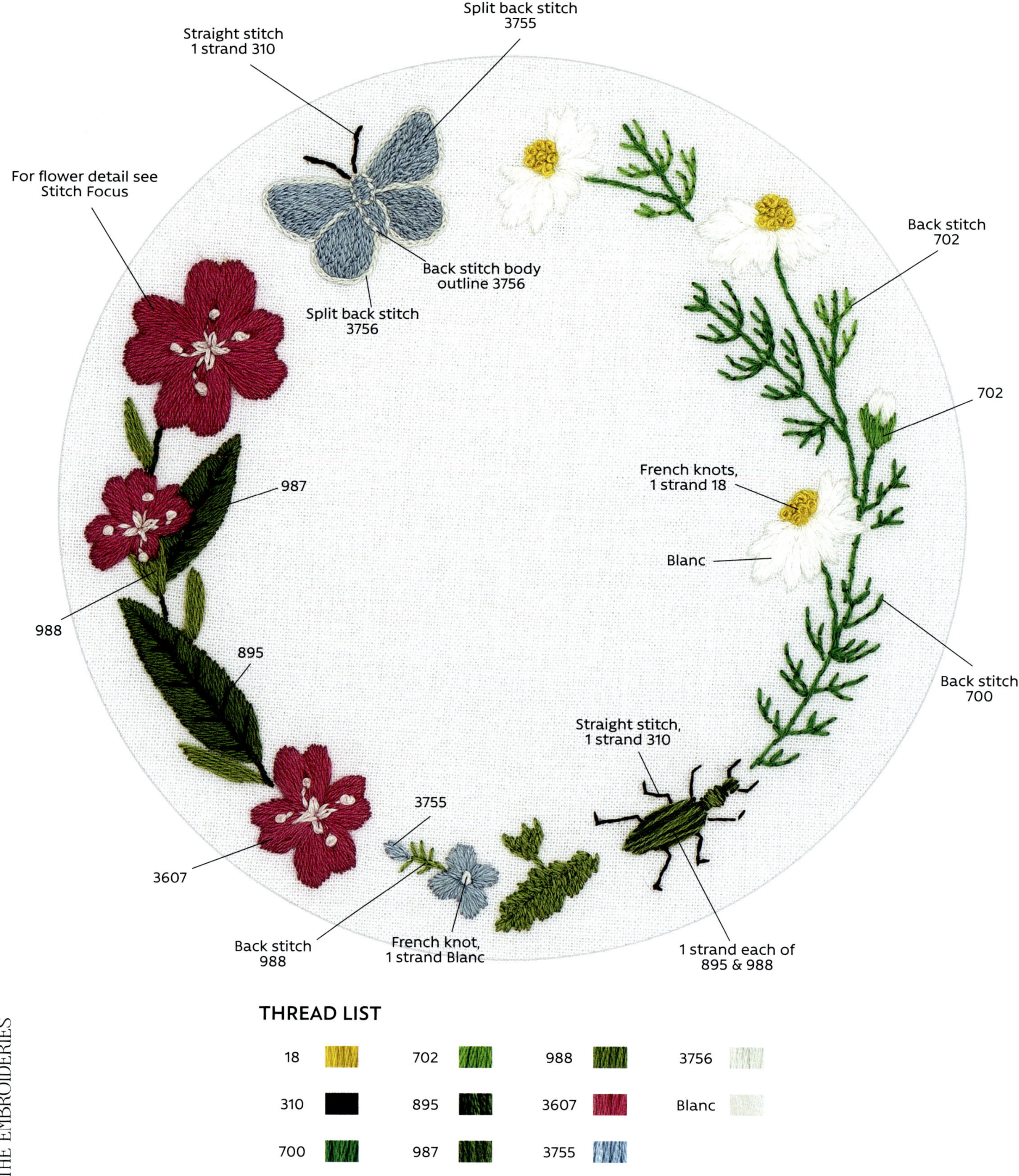

THREAD LIST

18		702		988		3756	
310		895		3607		Blanc	
700		987		3755			

STITCH FOCUS

The flowers of the great willow herb are so beautiful that it's hard to believe it's considered a weed in formal gardens! Here, satin stitch (3607) radiates to the edge of the petals. The centre of the flower is defined with lazy daisy stitches (Blanc), and the stamens are worked using just one strand, with a straight stitch ending in a French knot (Blanc).

The common blue butterfly is the most widespread blue butterfly in Britain and Ireland. Drinking nectar from a variety of flat-headed flowers, common blues sequester flavonoids from their host plants and allocate these UV-absorbing pigments into their wings. Their caterpillars secrete nutrient-containing substances that attract ants, and the ants protect the caterpillar from predators and probably tend the chrysalis too.

Block B4

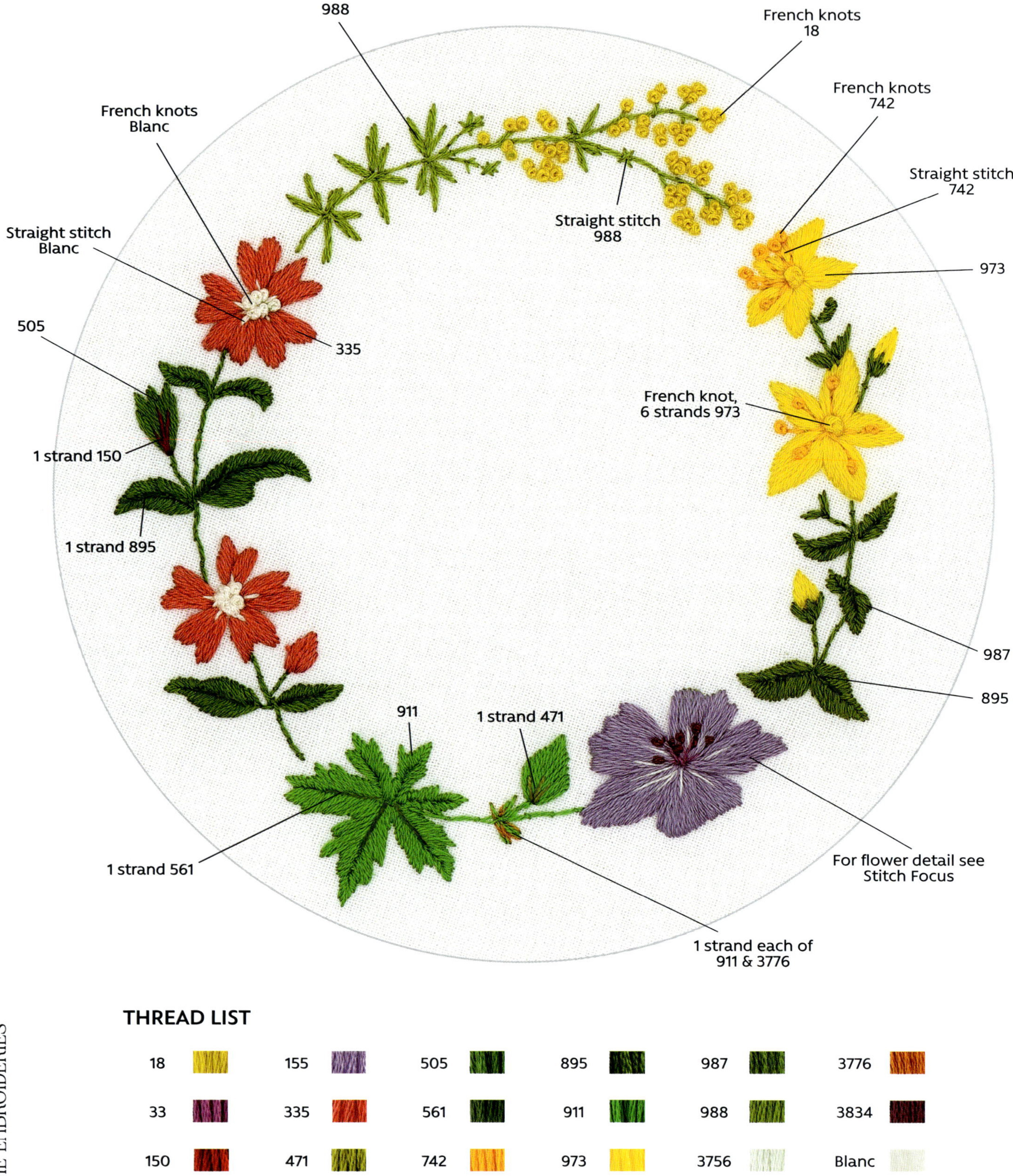

THREAD LIST

18	155	505	895	987	3776
33	335	561	911	988	3834
150	471	742	973	3756	Blanc

STITCH FOCUS

The blue-violet flowers of the meadow cranesbill are first stitched with satin stitch using two strands of 155, then one strand of 3756 for the grooves on the petals. Then detail stitching is worked on top: for the stamens at the very centre (see diagram), use one strand of 33 for the straight stitches and one strand of 3834 for the French knots.

The flowers of the lady's bedstraw can be used to make a pleasant tea. Member plants of the bedstraw family were traditionally used to stuff pillows and mattresses as they contain large amounts of coumarin, the molecule responsible for the wonderful scent of freshly mown hay – perfect to waft you off to a good night's sleep!

Block B5

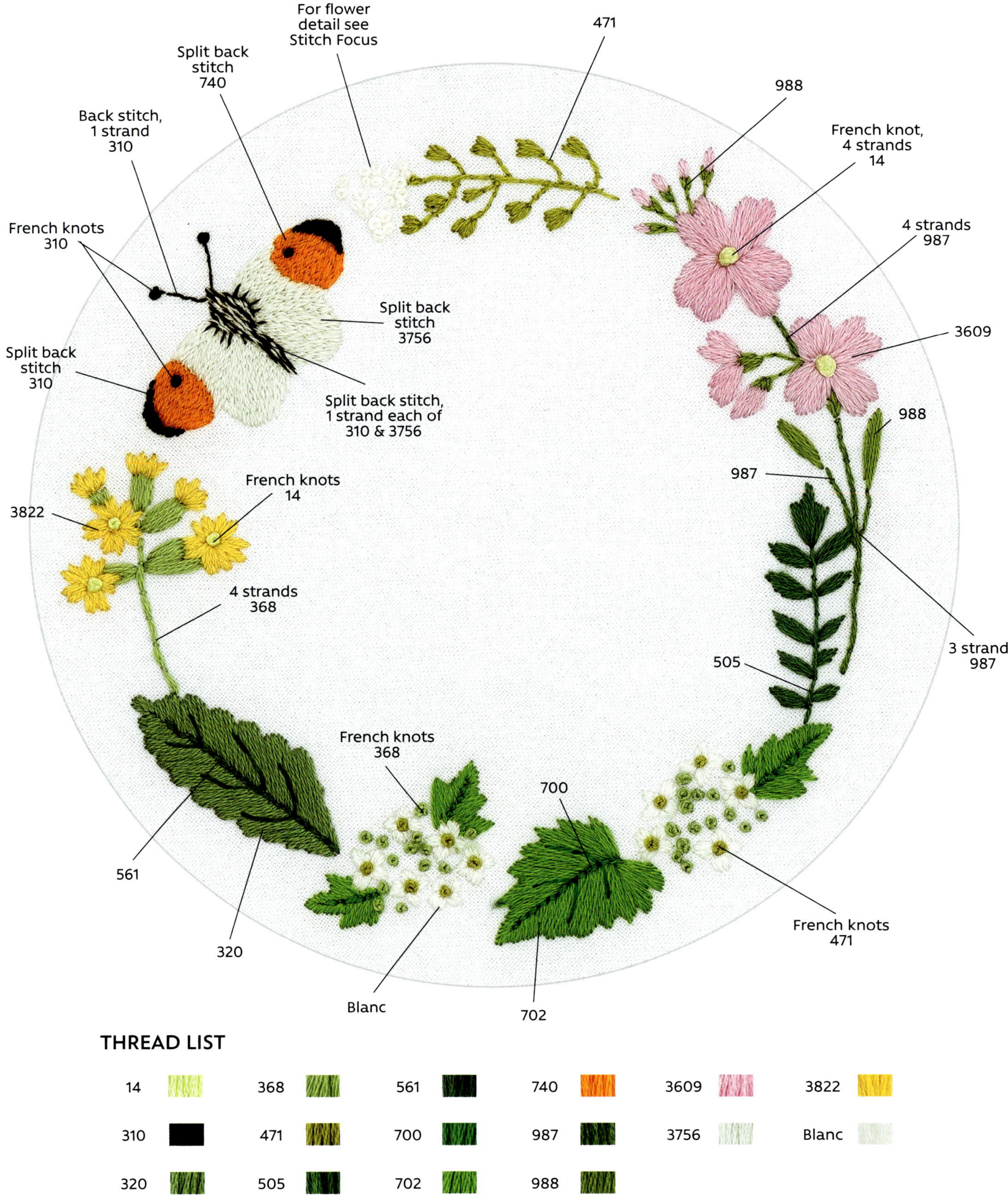

THREAD LIST

14	368	561	740	3609	3822
310	471	700	987	3756	Blanc
320	505	702	988		

STITCH FOCUS

The flowers of the field pennycress are created with French knots arranged as shown, using four strands of Blanc in the needle.

Usually one of the first species to emerge from the chrysalis in spring, the orange-tip butterfly lays its eggs on the cuckoo flower and garlic mustard, which are the food source of its caterpillars. These plants are considered weeds if found in the garden, but let them be if you want to be treated to the sight of these lovely butterflies. Garlic mustard leaves finish a risotto nicely, while the cuckoo flower has a sensational horseradish-like taste that will give you a tingly nose!

FLORA AND FAUNA KEY

1 Orange-tip butterfly

2 Field pennycress

3 Cuckoo flower (lady's smock)

4 Garlic mustard

5 Cowslip

Block B6

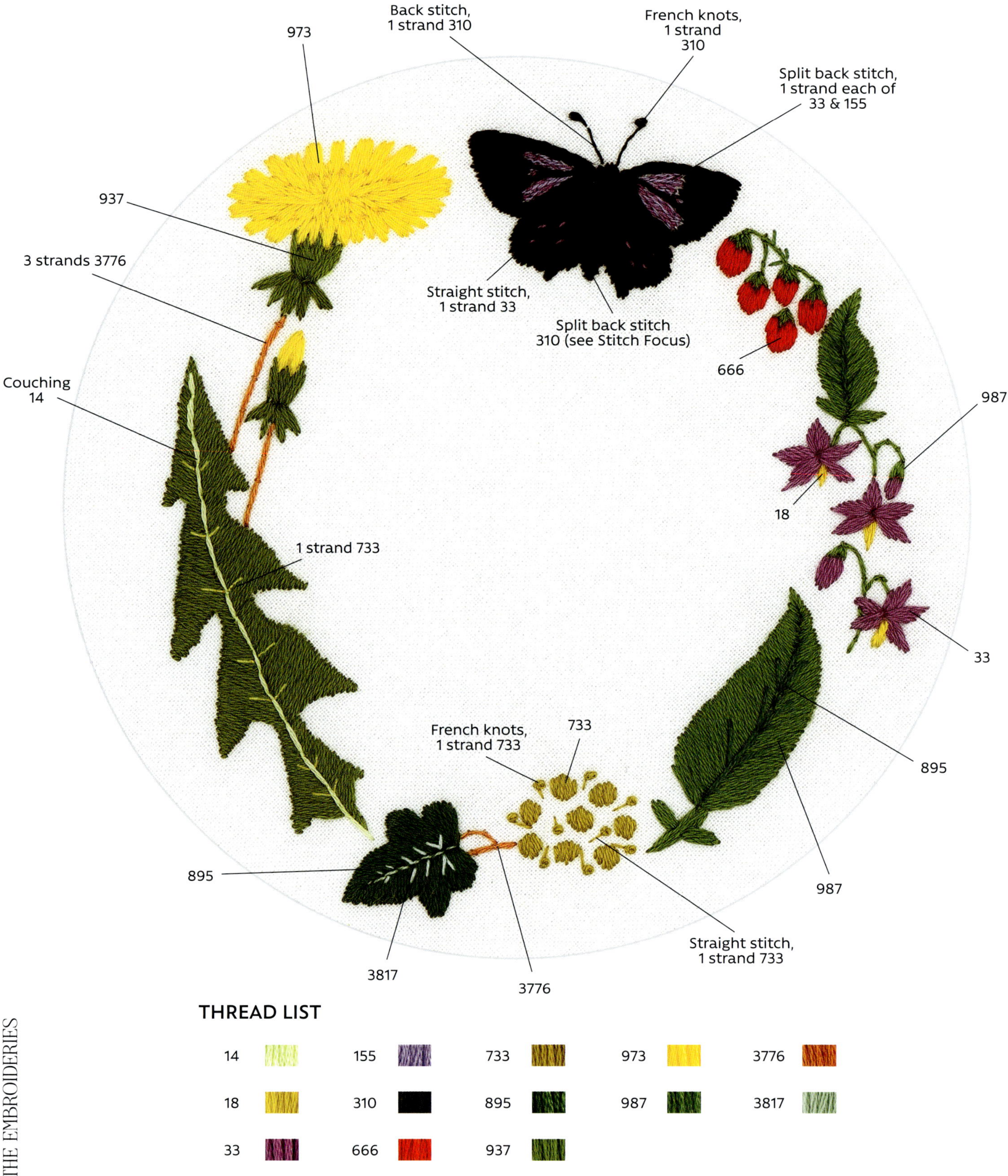

THREAD LIST

14		155		733		973		3776	
18		310		895		987		3817	
33		666		937					

STITCH FOCUS

Split back stitch is used for the background fill stitch of the butterfly. However, the direction of the stitching can be difficult to see on the black (310) areas of the design, so this diagram is provided to assist you and the grey lines indicate stitch direction. The purple lines on the lower wing indicate the single straight stitches that are worked on top with one strand of 33 once the background stitching is complete.

I often chomp on dandelion leaves on walks and they are a particular favourite of our guinea pigs! Dandelion improves liver and gall bladder function; it is frequently used to prevent or treat different liver diseases because of its rich composition in phytochemicals.

Block B7

THREAD LIST

155	471	895	3822
310	505	988	3834
368	742	3801	Blanc

STITCH FOCUS

To recreate the star-like flowers of the bog stitchwort, first embroider the petals with satin stitch using Blanc then add the remaining details following the diagram to render them perfectly in stitch.

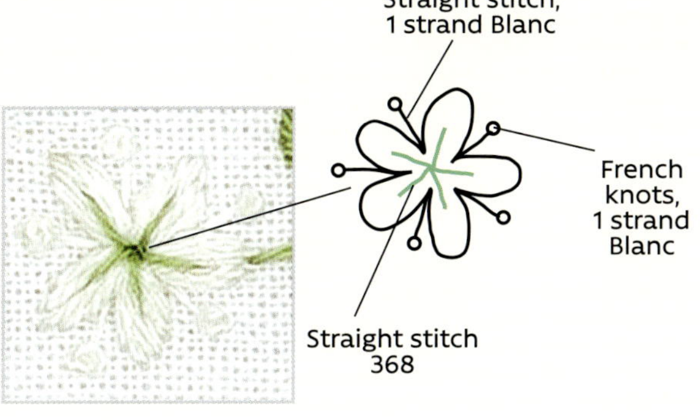

Ragwort is a particular favourite of the cinnabar moth and caterpillar – a female cinnabar moth can lay up to 300 eggs on the plant in batches of between thirty and sixty! Although the cinnabar moth is predominantly nocturnal, it can sometimes be seen in the day with its striking red-and-black colourway, from which it gets its name, after the mineral cinnabar, a toxic red ore of mercury that used to be made into beautiful carvings in China.

1 Ragwort

2 Cinnabar moth

3 Bugle

4 Bog stitchwort

5 Cinnabar caterpillar

Block B8

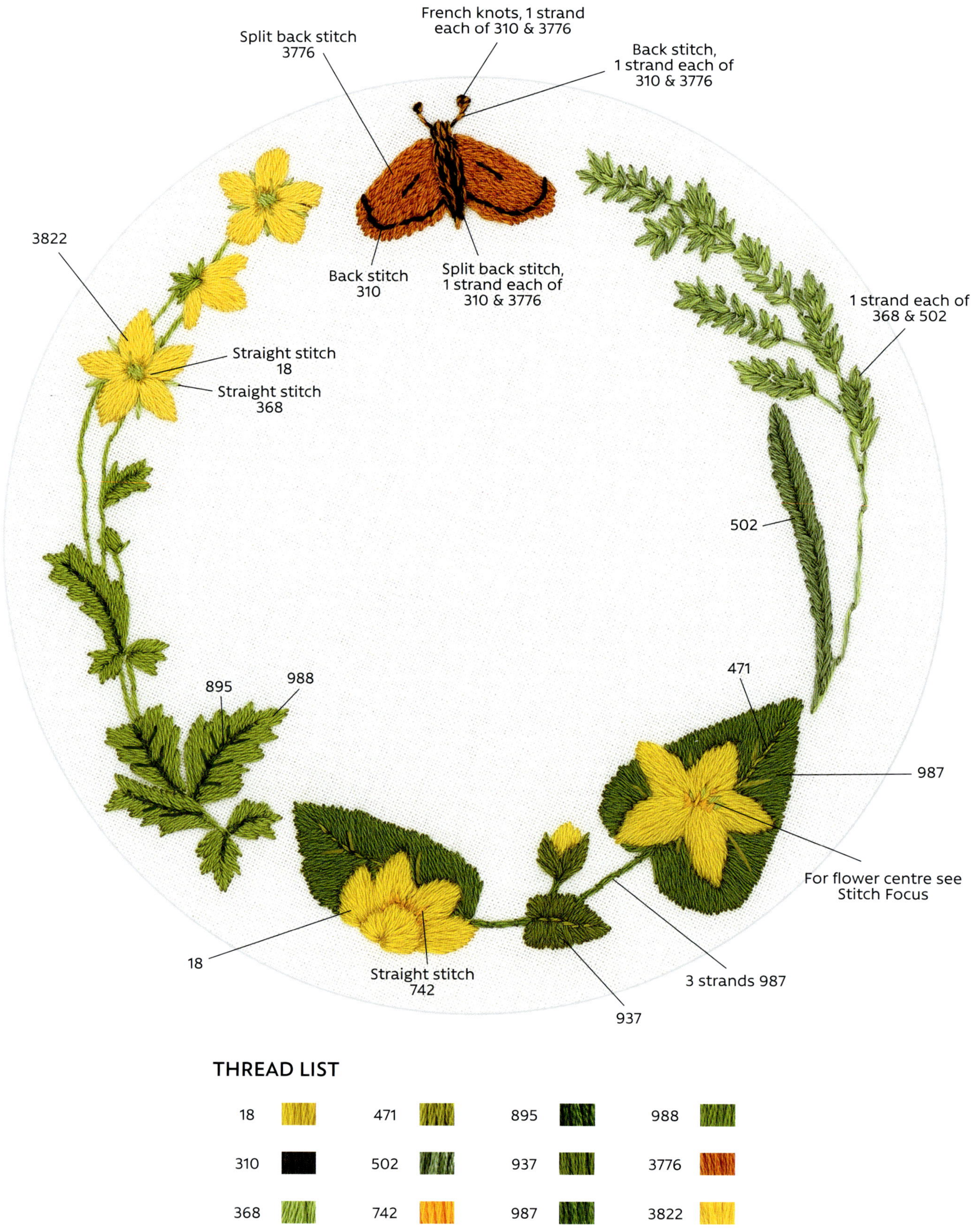

THREAD LIST

18	471	895	988
310	502	937	3776
368	742	987	3822

STITCH FOCUS

To work the centre detail of the full flower of the king cup (also known as the marsh marigold), first stitch a few single straight stitches on top of the satin stitch using 368, then work single straight stitches to surround them using 742.

Small skipper butterflies are widespread throughout the British mainland and are often seen darting around through tall grasses, particularly Yorkshire fog, which is the main food plant of the caterpillars. While I have long appreciated the wide variety of grasses that there are, I am only just beginning to learn some of their names!

FLORA AND FAUNA KEY

1 Small skipper butterfly

2 Yorkshire fog

3 King cup

4 Wood avens

Block B9

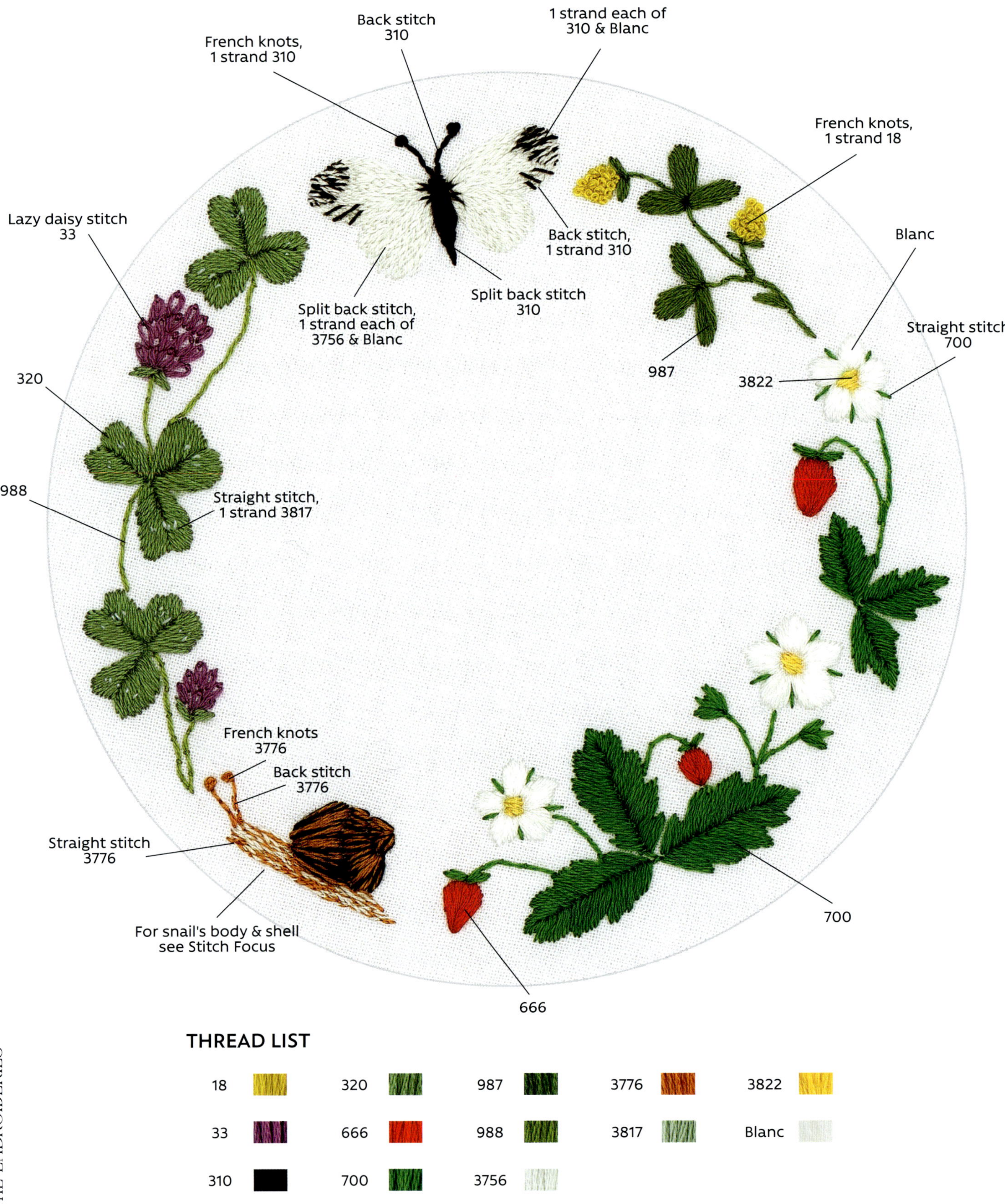

THREAD LIST

18	320	987	3776	3822
33	666	988	3817	Blanc
310	700	3756		

STITCH FOCUS

Garden snails may play havoc with your strawberry plants but they have an important role as nutrient recyclers and as prey for many species of birds. The snail is worked with split back stitch, using one strand each of 3756 and 3776 for the body and one strand each of 310 and 3776 for the shell.

Clover is an abundant staple of pasture land where it provides protein and nutrients for livestock. As a child, I used to love pulling the petals out and sucking on the tiny drops of sweet nectar. Scientific analysis has shown that red clover contains isoflavones, which have potential in the treatment of several conditions associated with menopause, such as hot flushes, cardiovascular health and osteoporosis.

Block B10

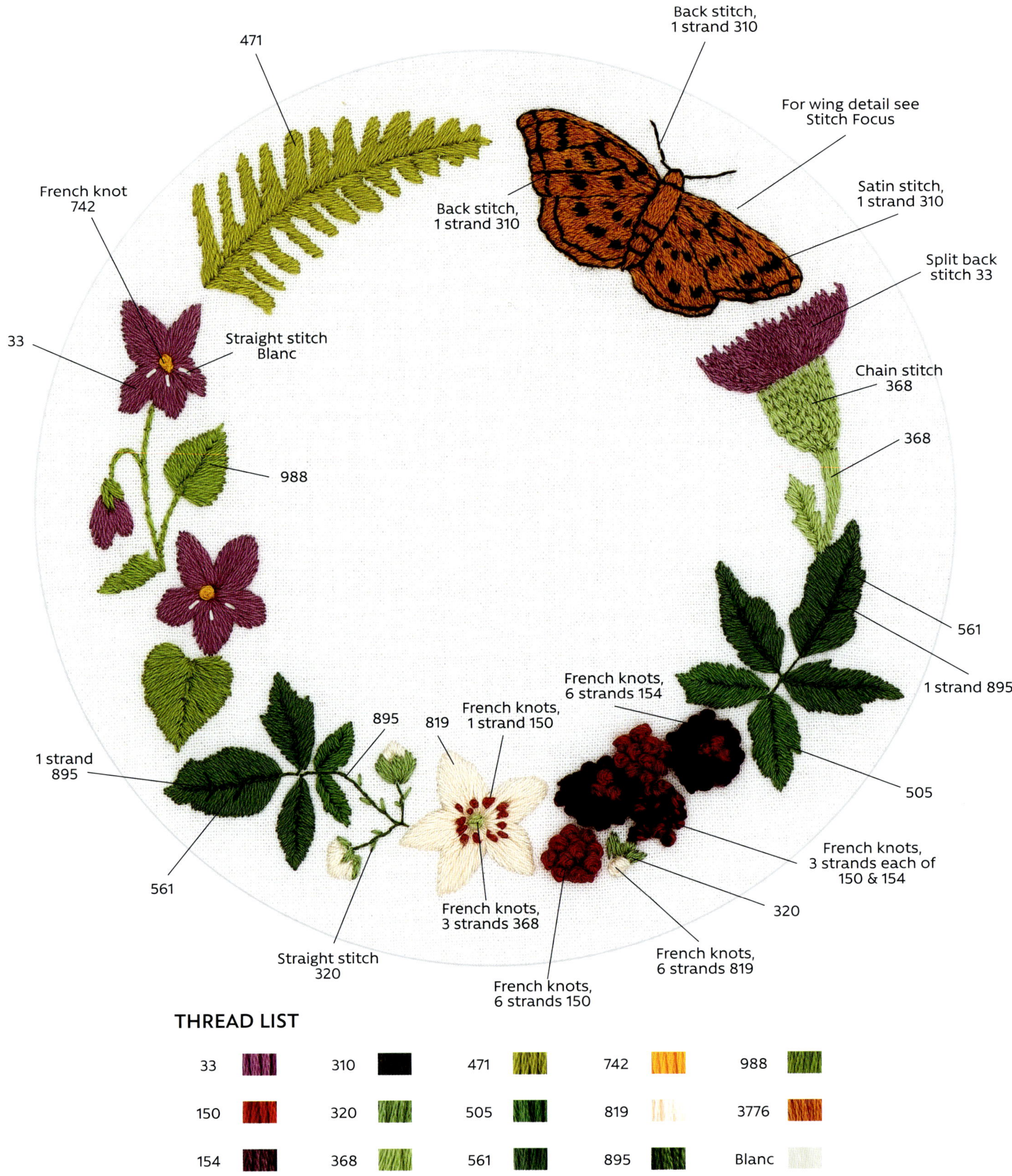

THREAD LIST

33	310	471	742	988
150	320	505	819	3776
154	368	561	895	Blanc

STITCH FOCUS

Follow the diagram to stitch the background detail of the butterfly wings first, using split back stitch to fill in direction indicated on the diagram with two strands of 3776. Then complete the pattern markings on top with one strand of 310, using satin stitch and back stitch.

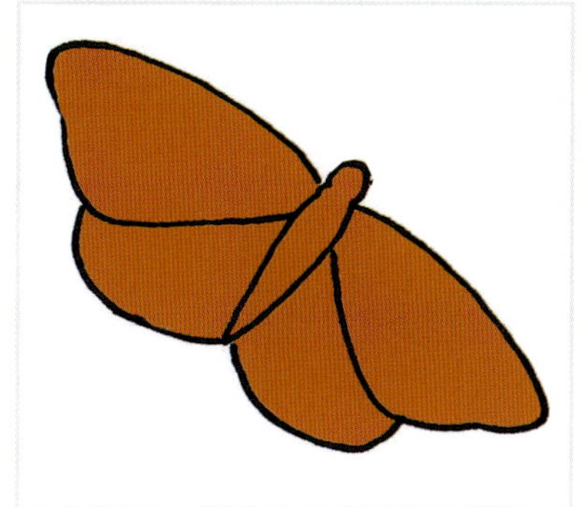

The tiny dog violet inhabits woodland edges, grassland and shady hedge banks. In the language of flowers, violets symbolise devotion yet these blooms, which appear in early spring, can last for just a few days! The leaves and flowers are edible raw or cooked and can be used to make violet sugar or sorbet.

Block B11

THREAD LIST

14	368	937	988	3776	3834
33	471	986	3755	3822	Blanc
310	740	987	3756		

STITCH FOCUS

When stitching the tortoiseshell butterfly, you might find it useful to follow this diagram to achieve its symmetrical markings with satin stitch. Once the background stitching is complete, the French knots on the outer edges of the wings are worked on top using just one strand of 3755.

The bee orchid is a sneaky mimic: the flower's velvety lip looks like a female bee, so males fly in to try to mate with it and end up pollinating the flower. In the UK, this orchid is self-pollinated as the right bee species doesn't live here. While the bee orchid is not classified as rare, the only place I have seen them is in the sand dunes of a beach in west Wales!

Block B12

THREAD LIST

14	335	702	988	3776	3834
310	505	986	3609	3817	Blanc
320	700	987	3756		

STITCH FOCUS

The pretty pink flowers of the sorrel plant are achieved by using one strand each of 335 and 3609 in the needle.

Autumn crocus, also known as meadow saffron, is a plant of damp hay meadows and woodland rides and clearings, but it's popular in gardens too. Be aware, however, that it is a highly toxic plant, from which colchicine can be extracted and used in small doses for the treatment of gout.

Block B13

For wing detail see Stitch Focus

3756

3047

French knots, 3 strands 3817

Back stitch 310

French knots 14

3822

502

310

French knot 18

3817

Blanc

3609

18

702

700

THREAD LIST

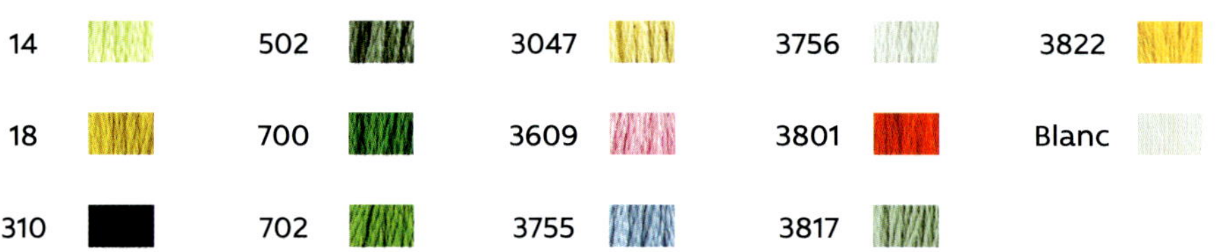

14	502	3047	3756	3822
18	700	3609	3801	Blanc
310	702	3755	3817	

STITCH FOCUS

The swallowtail is the UK's largest butterfly: when stitching the exotic beauty of its wings, start by using split back stitch to fill the background detail areas first, as shown in this diagram.

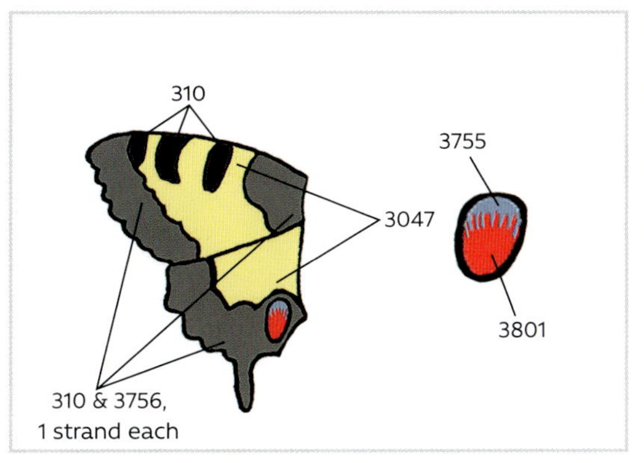

In the language of flowers agrimony means 'thankfulness' or 'gratefulness'. I discovered agrimony a few years ago, around the time that I also decided to integrate daily gratitude practice into my life. Agrimony appears in fair abundance in fields that have been rewilded. It's also found along hedgerows and has a long flowering time, all through the summer and into September.

Block B14

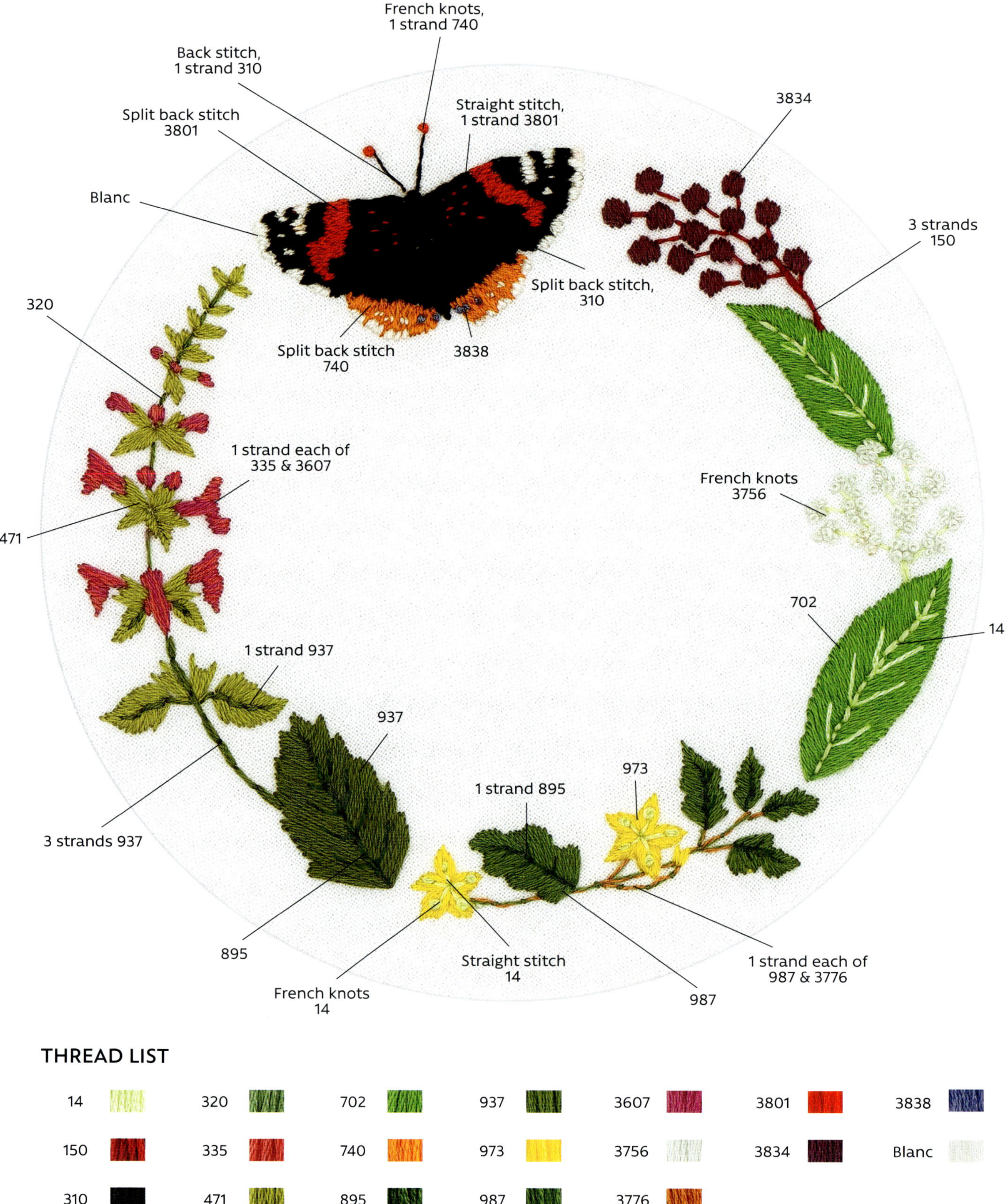

THREAD LIST

14	320	702	937	3607	3801	3838
150	335	740	973	3756	3834	Blanc
310	471	895	987	3776		

STITCH FOCUS

When embroidering the red admiral, it's important to carefully observe the direction of stitching of the 310 split back stitch on the wings (as indicated by the grey lines in this diagram). Also take care with the placing of the Blanc and 3838 satin stitch details, particularly the Blanc worked around the edges of the wings. This diagram will help you to achieve accuracy in your stitching.

Woundworts contain the phytochemical germacrene D, which has antibacterial and antifungal properties. Hedge woundwort is good for dealing with inflammation and swelling, and also excellent for managing pain. It was widely used in the Middle Ages, especially when treating the wounded on the battlefield. Elizabeth Blackwell in her beautifully illustrated book A Curious Herbal *(published c.1737) records it's use in the treatment of all sorts of wounds (especially infected ones) as well as to help stop internal bleeding.*

FLORA AND FAUNA KEY

1 Red admiral butterfly

2 Elderberry

3 Yellow pimpernel

4 Hedge woundwort

Block B15

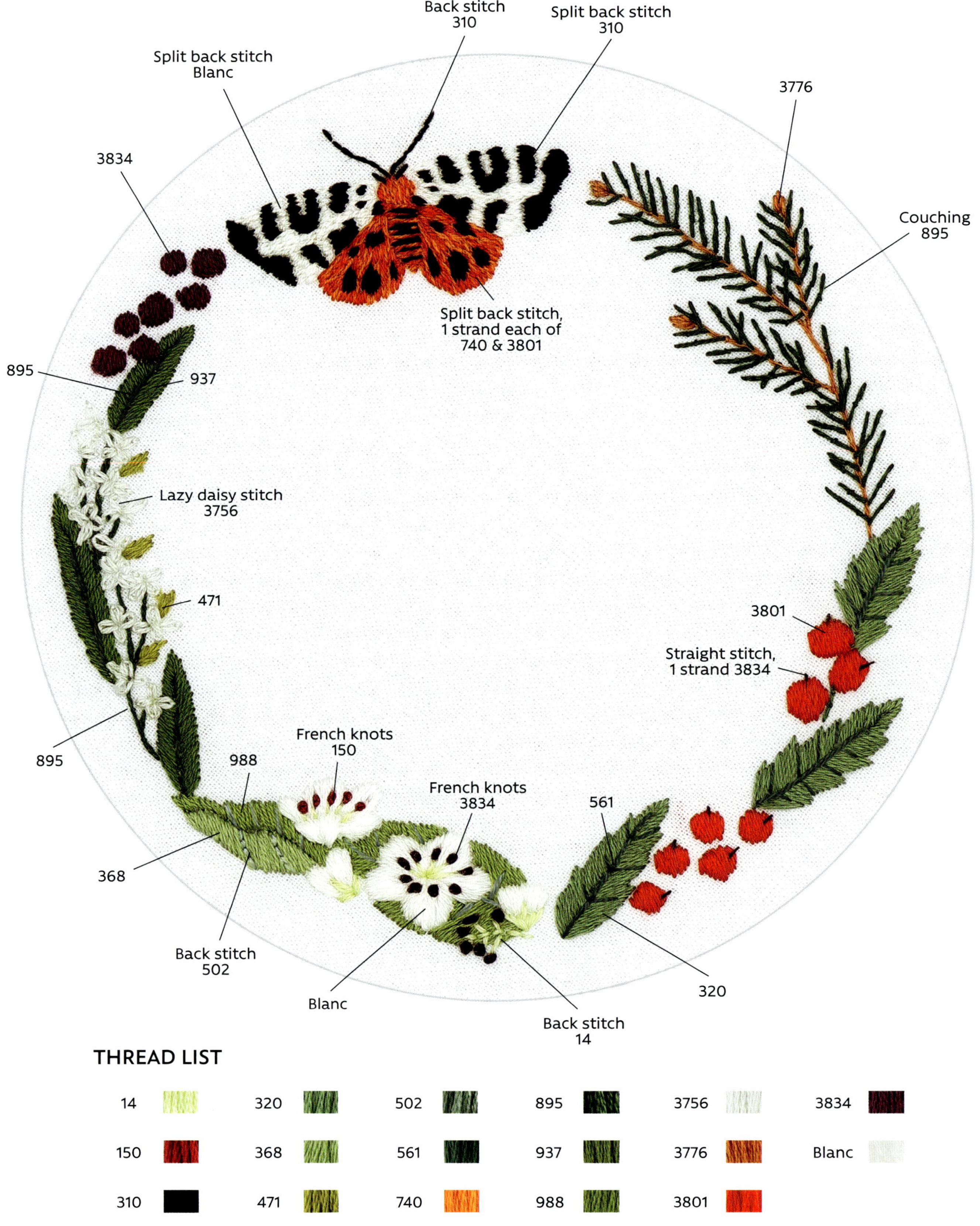

THREAD LIST

14	320	502	895	3756	3834
150	368	561	937	3776	Blanc
310	471	740	988	3801	

STITCH FOCUS

The distinctive markings of the garden tiger moth are achieved by working split back stitch in 310 over the background stitching of the wings. The wings are also worked in split back stitch using Blanc for the upper wings and one strand each of 3801 and 740 for the lower wings, head and body, paying particular attention to the direction of the stitching on the head and body.

The Douglas fir is an evergreen conifer that can live for more than a thousand years. As they are so long-lived, these trees provide deadwood cavities for birds and bats to shelter in; being tall, they also make perfect nesting sites for larger birds of prey. Douglas fir timber is of great commercial importance for building, and they are widely grown as Christmas trees.

FLORA AND FAUNA KEY

1 Garden tiger moth

2 Douglas fir

3 Rowan (mountain ash)

4 Wild pear

5 Privet

Block B16

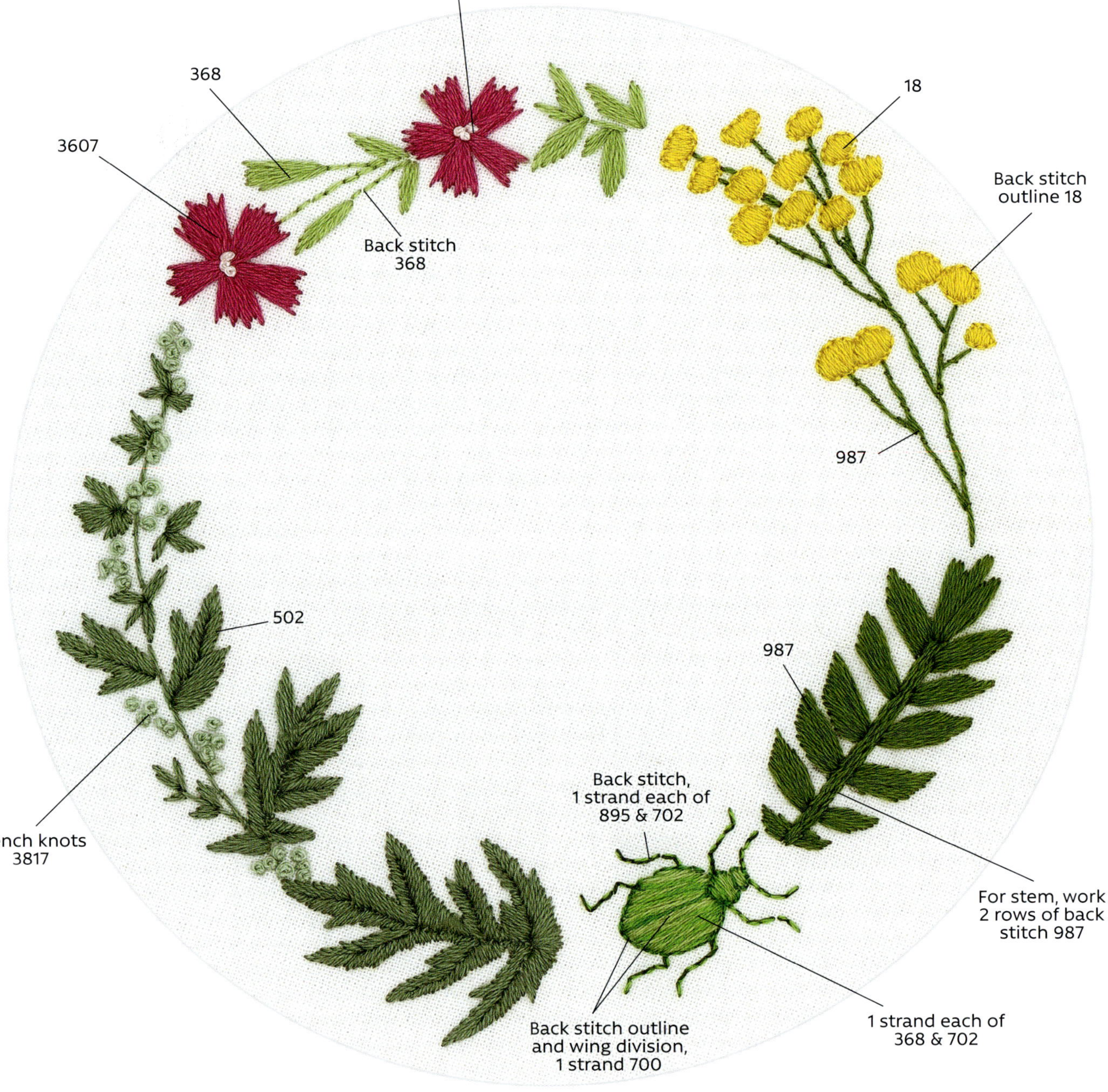

French knots,
1 strand Blanc

368

3607

18

Back stitch
outline 18

Back stitch
368

987

502

987

French knots
3817

Back stitch,
1 strand each of
895 & 702

For stem, work
2 rows of back
stitch 987

Back stitch outline
and wing division,
1 strand 700

1 strand each of
368 & 702

THREAD LIST

18	700	987	3817
368	702	3607	Blanc
502	895		

STITCH FOCUS

To faithfully replicate the UK's 'Nationally Rare' tansy beetle in satin stitch, use one strand each of 368 and 702 in the needle carefully following the direction indicated in the diagram, then use one strand of 700 and back stitch to outline the beetle's shape and the different parts of its body.

*With its gentle appealing fragrance and pretty flowers, maiden pink dianthus is ideal for decorating cakes and salads. Most dianthus have a pleasant spicy, floral, clove-like taste, especially the more fragrant varieties. My Mum used to grow carnations (*Dianthus caryophyllus*) in her market garden. The scent reminds me of childhood summers.*

ABOUT THE AUTHOR

Alice has always loved playing with fabrics, finding particular joy in combining colours. Finding a snippet of Liberty amongst her grandmother's quilting stash of worn out dresses and vintage fabrics was always a highlight and from there her passion for Liberty fabrics grew.

Trained in scientific research, she kept her passion for sewing alive throughout her Ph.D in genetics, selling handmade bags at student fairs. It was from here that she started her business, Alice Caroline. Alice now enjoys running her business and designing sewing patterns and kits, which are stocked in the iconic Liberty of London store. Alice Caroline specialises in Liberty fabrics, sending Liberty fabrics, patterns and kits all over the world.

In her Country Diary Quilt, Alice brings together her scientific curiosity and her love of design; it features twenty-five embroidered blocks celebrating British wildflowers. Each one is stitched with an eye for beauty yet also rooted in research, drawing on the history, folklore and medicinal stories of the plants. Her work celebrates the meeting place of science and creativity, keeping alive both the heritage of quilt-making and the wonder of the natural world.

Alice lives and works in the rolling countryside of Gloucestershire, in the UK.

LIBERTY FABRIC STOCKISTS

UK

Alice Caroline
www.alicecaroline.com
Liberty Fabric specialist with a huge range of classic, seasonal and exclusive Liberty prints. Free worldwide shipping options. Alice's Country Diary Quilt kits and related products available.

Instagram: @alicecarolinefabrics
Pinterest: @alicecaroline
Facebook: Alice Caroline Liberty Fabric
YouTube: @alicecarolinefabrics
TikTok: @alicecarolinefabrics

Liberty London
www.libertylondon.com

Sew & Quilt
www.sewandquilt.co.uk

AUSTRALIA & NEW ZEALAND

Tessuti
www.tessuti-shop.com

The Fabric Store
www.thefabricstoreonline.com

Annie's Country Quilt Store
www.anniesquilts.co.nz

EUROPE

Stragier
www.stragier.com

Telerie Spadari Milano
www.teleriespadari.it

Gårda Textil
www.gardatextil.se

USA

Jones &Vandermeer
www.jonesandvandermeer.com

Morris Textiles
www.morristextiles.com

The Intrepid Thread
www.intrepidthread.com

JAPAN

Liberty Japan
www.liberty-japan.co.jp

Lilymeru
www.lilymeru.etsy.com

ChokiChoki22
www.chokichoki22.etsy.com

GENERAL FABRICS & HABERDASHERY

Please support your local fabric shop in the first instance where possible. They may not have Liberty in particular, but they will undoubtably have your necessary haberdashery, DMC embroidery threads, as well as cotton quilting fabrics for you to coo over!

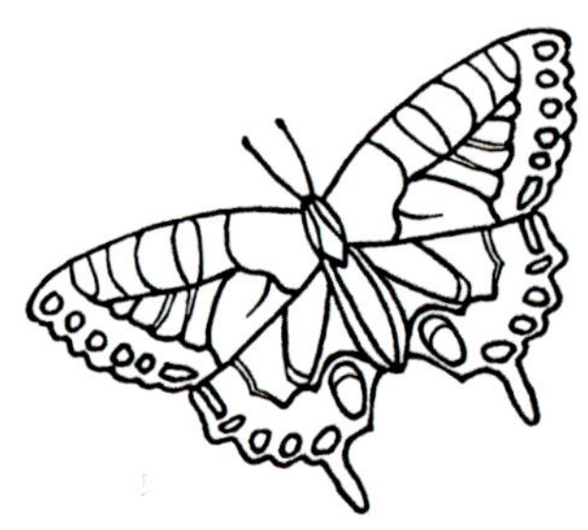

INDEX

A DAVID AND CHARLES BOOK

David and Charles is an imprint of David and Charles, Ltd
Suite A, Tourism House, Pynes Hill, Exeter, EX2 5WS

EU GPSR Authorised Representative:
Logos Europe, 9 rue Nicolas Poussin, 17000, La Rochelle, France
Email: Contact@logoseurope.eu

First published in the UK and USA in 2026

A catalogue record for this book is available from the British Library.

ISBN-13: 9781446317310 hardback
ISBN-13: 9781446317327 EPUB

This book has been printed on paper from approved suppliers and made from pulp from sustainable sources.

Printed in China by Asia Pacific Offset for:
David and Charles, Ltd
Suite A, Tourism House, Pynes Hill, Exeter, EX2 5WS

10 9 8 7 6 5 4 3 2 1

Publishing Director: Ame Verso
Publishing Manager: Jeni Chown
Editor: Victoria Allen
Project Editor: Cheryl Brown
Lead Designer: Sam Staddon
Designer: Jess Pearson and Jo Webb
Pre-press Designer: Susan Reansbury
Illustrations: Alice Garrett and Laura Enriquez
Art Direction: Prudence Rogers
Photography: Jason Jenkins
Production Manager: Beverley Richardson

Full-size printable versions of the transfers are available to download free from www.bookmarkedhub.com. Search for this book by the title or ISBN: the files can be found under 'Book Extras'. Membership of the Bookmarked online community is free.

David and Charles publishes high-quality books on a wide range of subjects. For more information visit www.davidandcharles.com.

Share your makes with us on social media using #dandcbooks and follow us on Facebook and Instagram by searching for @dandcbooks.

Layout of the digital edition of this book may vary depending on reader hardware and display settings.

THANKS

This book would simply not exist without the immense dedication of Laura Enriquez, who did an extraordinary amount of work, writing and designing with such clarity and care. I am endlessly grateful for her commitment and generosity of spirit.

A huge thank you to Anna Sanders, who brought the quilt to life so beautifully with her many hours of stitching. Thank you also to Alison Eaton, whose embroidery work is also featured in these pages. I'm also thankful to Kate and Dawn for their stitching help along the way. Thank you to Jo at Loulourioux for her beautiful long arm quilting. I am deeply grateful to the wonderful team at Alice Caroline, whose constant support and behind-the-scenes work make projects like this possible.

Finally, my heartfelt thanks go to the wonderful team at David & Charles, whose expertise and enthusiasm and belief in this project brought the book to life.

The Embroidery Transfers

Iron-on transfers for both the stitch sampler and all the embroideries featured in Alice's Country Diary Quilt are conveniently provided here, ready for you to use. Carefully tear along the perforated edge and follow the instructions in Embroidery Techniques: Transfer the Patterns for how to transfer the designs to your fabric.

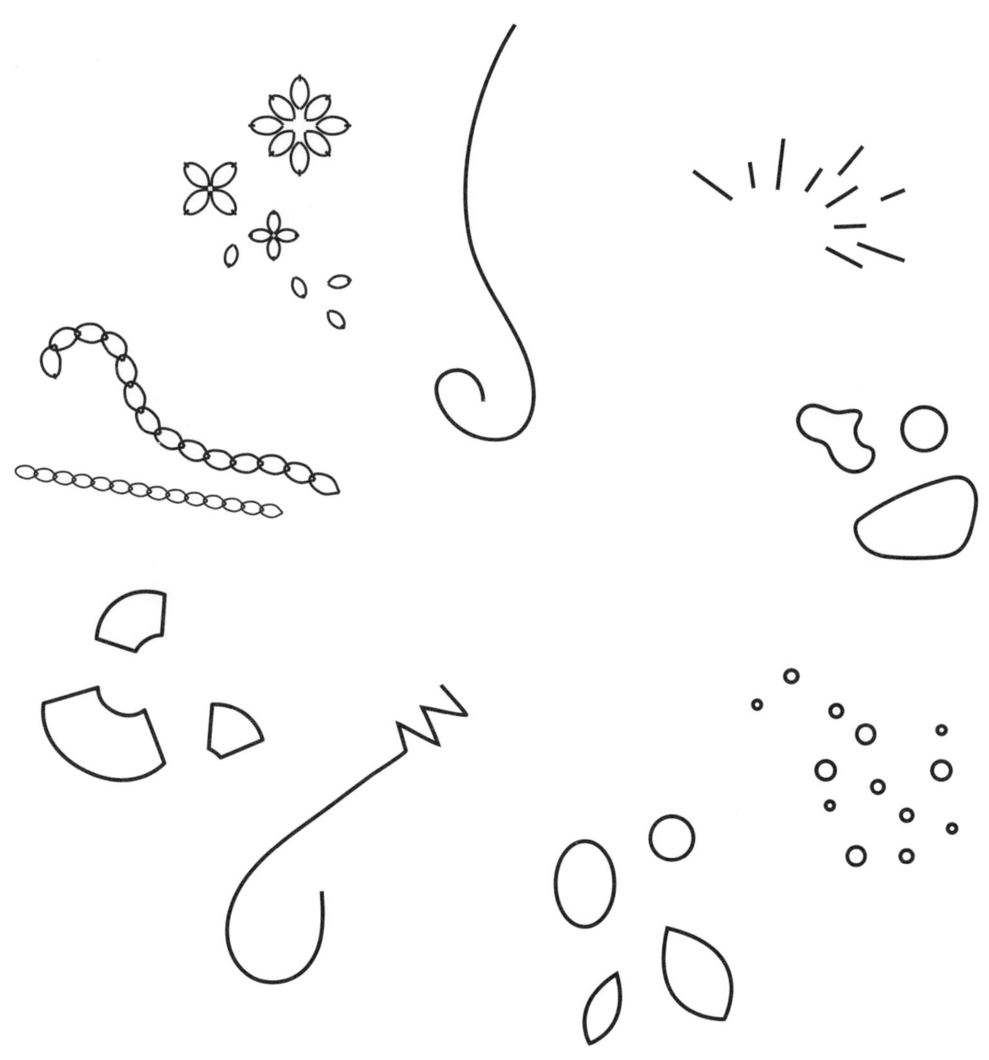

BLOCK A3

BLOCK A4

BLOCK B1